minimalism

maximalism

From minimalism to maximalism

Editor: **Paco Asensio**

Author: **Aurora Cuito**

Text on furniture: **Cristina Montes**

Translation: **Edward William Krasny**

Art Director: **Mireia Casanovas Soley**

Graphic Design and Layout: **Emma Termes Parera**

2002 © Loft Publications S.L. and HBI,
an imprint of HarperCollins International

First published in 2002 by LOFT and HBI,
an imprint of HarperCollins International
10 East 53rd St., New York, NY 10022-5299

Distributed in the U.S. and Canada by Watson-Guptill Publications
770 Broadway, New York, NY 10003-9595
Telephone: (800) 451-1741 or (732) 363-4511 in NJ, AK, HI Fax: (732) 363-0338

Distributed throughout the rest of the world by
HarperCollins International
10 East 53rd St. New York, NY 10022-5299
Fax: (212) 207-7654

ISBN HBI edition: 0-06-051356-X
ISBN Watson-Guptill and HBI edition: 0-8230-3077-6
D.L.: B- 32.854-02

Editorial Project

LOFT Publications
Domènech, 9 2-2
08012 Barcelona. Spain
Tel.: +34 932 183 099
Fax: +34 932 370 060
e-mail: loft@loftpublications.com
www.loftpublications.com

Printed in:
Gráficas Anman. Sabadell, Spain

July 2002

If you would like to suggest projects for inclusion in our next volumes, please e-mail details to us at: loft@loftpublications.com

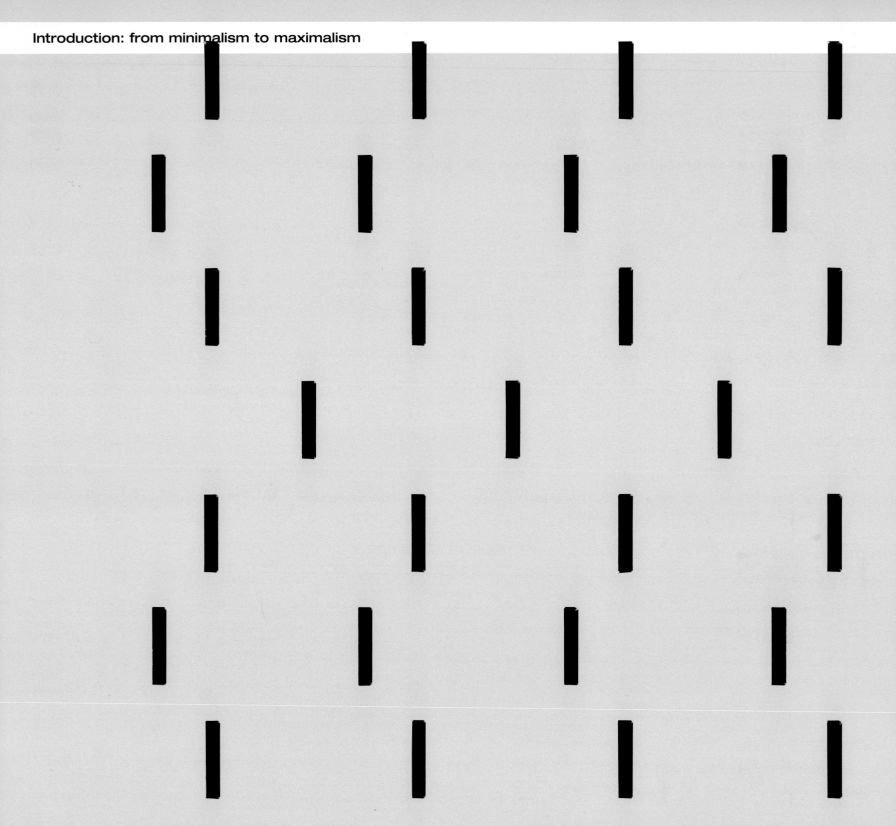

More is never enough

The successive artistic movements that have emerged over the course of history have alternated between periods of exuberance and restraint. This tendency to swing between sophistication and simplicity can be seen in a comparison of two currents as early as Romanesque and gothic art: the former generated straightforward, unadorned shapes dictated by a relatively primitive technology while the latter produced more complex geometries made possible by advances in constructional systems. One need only compare the church of Sant Climent in Taüll, in the Catalan Pyrenees, with the cathedral of Chartres, southwest of Paris, to see the great stylistic leap from the plainness of the former to the complexity of the latter.

This tendency repeats again and again in successive artistic currents, for example in the transformation of the simple lines of classicism into the profusion of ornamentation in baroque with its the buildings abounding in volutes, brackets, plinths and cornices. Likewise, in the early 20th century, the modern movement, which sought to economise on shapes and materials, precedes postmodernism, in which the right angle disappears and geometry gains complexity to yield a broad range of results. The latter current emerged in the eighties with the book "Complexity and Contradiction in Architecture" by the American architect Robert Venturi as its bible, advocating a world rich in materials, shapes and colours where the perception of the buildings becomes a festival for the senses. We come full cycle once again in the early nineties with the birth of minimalism, a tendency which sought to offer a respite following the opulence of postmodernism and deconstructivism. Despite being subject to a variety of interpretations –as an inheritance of Cistercian architecture, as an evolution of the artistic lines of the sixties, as a reading of Japanese austerity– minimalism has always been materialized according to the same scheme: the reduction of art to basic concepts of space, light and mass. This inclination to pursue simplicity became a fashion, and shades of white, right angles and subtlety as a design strategy were exploited to the hilt, saturating creators and consumers alike. In response to this saturation, a new system of creation artistic emerged, reflecting the need to forge a more complex art. Clients and designers strive to reproduce their needs, wants and even their caprices in their projects. After a ten-year-plus reign of austerity an aesthetic shift celebrating variety and plurality is being experienced with gusto.

This new sensitivity, which in this work we have been so bold as to label "maximalism", encompasses the intentions of designers who are constructing a new complex and eclectic modernity.

As occurs with any aesthetic trend that erupts with force, maximalism has had a major impact on all disciplines, even fostering certain bastardisation and the emergence of new multidisciplinary fields. Fashion design, as ever on the leading edge, was one of the first realms in which maximalism began to show its face. Calvinist clothing has vanished from the catwalks giving way to models that combine varied materials: leather, patent leather, gauze and studs impregnate the wear of firms such Dolce & Gabbana, Versace and Vivienne Westwood. Even the serenity of Giorgio Armani has been disturbed with the incorporation of opulent and showy fabrics.

Industrial design is also undergoing transformation: in furniture comfort is no longer enough, and originality through singular shapes and colours is sought after as well. Wave-shaped shelves, fuzzy sofas, curvy-legged tables, animal-shaped tin openers... an endless list of objects which surprise us with their blend of functionality and imagination.

Maximalism has also transformed such disciplines as jewellery-making, film, literature and graphic design, now governed by conceptual and technical tools which pursue ambiguities, tensions and transgressive orders.

Architecture is, however, the discipline in which these changes are most perceptible and in some cases most exaggerated. Architects have abandoned the heretofore-omnipresent white-painted reinforced concrete and begun to erect their buildings with a fusion of new materials such as corrugated metal panels and glass capable of changing translucence in a matter of seconds. No longer is ornamentation a sin; fabrics, sophisticated finishes, combinations of antique and futuristic furnishings make for atmospheres rich in sensations where the sole but sufficient utility is beauty.

This book presents a first crop of maximalist projects in which the superposition of elements leads to greater richness and perfection. The careful selection of public buildings, commercial spaces and dwellings humbly contradicts Mies's maxim that "less is more" and shows that more is never enough.

DZ Bank

Peckham Library

Vocational Training Center

Expansion of the
Architecture School

Magna Science Museum

Hypo Alpe Adria Bank

Café Musiques

Spa Bad Elster

Mind Zone

The Lounge

Museum of Art and Technology

Museum of Extreme Culture

Queens Museum of Art

New Holland Cultural Center

Claesson Koivisto Rune **No Picnic Offices**

minimalist

DZ Bank

The DZ Bank building, located in the heart of Berlin, is a hybrid complex that accommodates residential and commercial uses. The commercial part houses the bank's main offices in the city and faces the Pariser Platz and the historic Brandenburg Gate. The residential area, comprising 39 flats, looks on to a quieter street, Behrenstrasse.

Both façades were erected with yellow limestone so that the color of the new construction would match the existing historic buildings. The composition of the enclosures was also adapted to the proportions of the neighboring buildings, in an attempt to create a singular, coherent urban environment. A good example of this strategy is the Pariser Platz façade, where the windows were set back in keeping with the adjacent buildings.

A large glass roof shelters the main entrance to the bank building. One passes under the glass hood and enters an enormous lobby from which one sees the centerpiece of the project: a spectacular interior atrium crowned with a vaulted roof, made of glass, as is the floor. The offices are arrayed around this grand courtyard to take advantage of the luminosity it offers. A series of wood-clad arcades lead to the elevators, located at either side of the atrium.

The main conference hall of the complex is located in a sculptured volume over the glass floor of the atrium, giving it the appearance of floating in space. The exterior of the body is of stainless steel and the interior is entirely panelled in wood, thus creating a warm and comfortable atmosphere for meetings. Other common rooms are in the basement arrayed around a large hall, where the café is also located. These spaces can be joined to accommodate large conventions or banquets.

The residential area is also centerd on a courtyard, which, though smaller, still affords the flats natural light on two sides. The water in a small pool on the ground floor produces numerous luminous effects, reflections and iridescences which can be seen from the glass corridors and elevators.

A range of residences was designed for the building, from small studios to a pair of luxurious top-floor duplexes with magnificent views of the city.

The DZ Bank is a project that combines masterfully numerous disciplines, architecture, sculpture and painting.

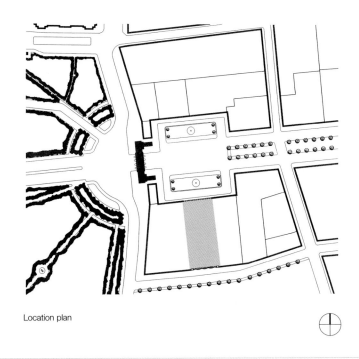

Location plan

The façade of the residences, overlooking a quiet street, acquires a singular character from the undulation of the facing. All the balconies, moreover, project at different angles from the plane, thus attaining a complex composition. The upper floors are set back to create small terraces.

The balconies of the residences are made of an aluminum skeleton and a glass railing riveted to the metal work. The volume projecting from the façade is enclosed in glass at the front and sides.

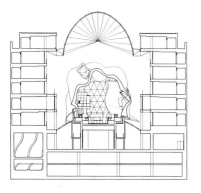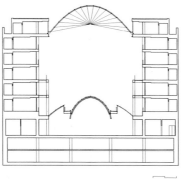

Cross sections

0 3 6

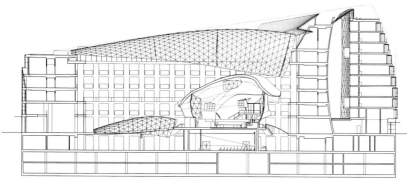

Longitudinal sections

0 4 8

The sections show clearly the formal complexity of the roof system of the courtyards. These geometries are generated with the aid of computer programes and the building of models, a method used profusely at the studio headed by Frank O. Gehry.

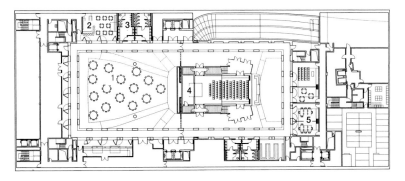

Basement

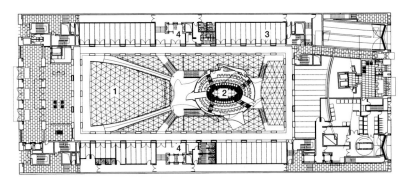

Ground floor

1. Café
2. Bar
3. Toilets
4. Auditorium
5. Conference hall

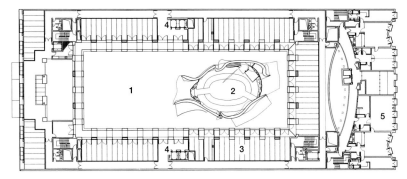

First floor

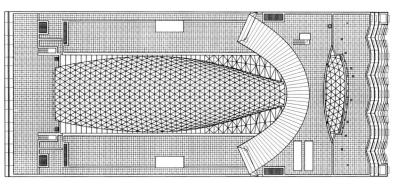

Roof plan

1. Courtyard
2. Conference hall
3. Offices
4. Elevators
5. Residences

0 1 2

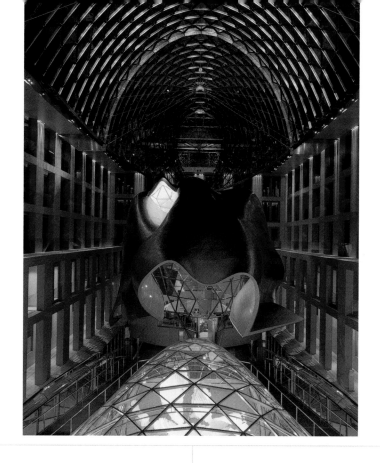

Architects: Gehry Partners, LLP

Collaborators: Ingenieur Büro Müuler Marl GmbH and Schlaich Bergermann und Partner (structures), Brandi Ingenieure GmbH (mechanical/electrical).

Built: 2001

Location: Berlin, Germany

Gross floor area: 215,053 sq. ft.

Photography: Roland Halbe

Photograph on page 14: Patrik Engquist

Carsten Roth **Optimal Library** **minimalist**

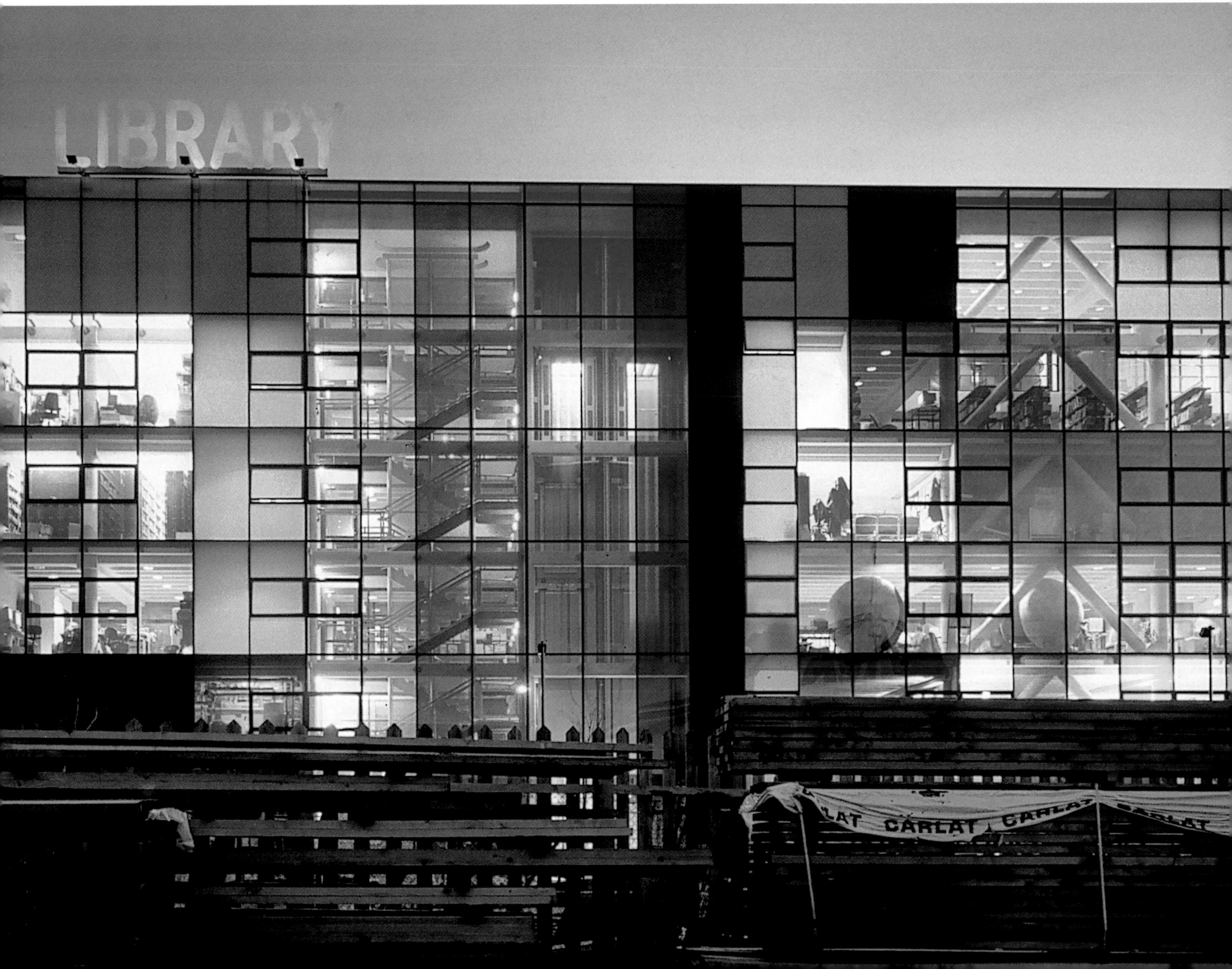
LIBRARY
CARLAT CARLAT

Peckham Library

This project is part of a major urban renewal program for the Peckham area in southeast London. In conjunction with other projects, such as the construction of a modern sports center in 1998 or the refurbishing of the urban furnishings, the library creates a new landscape.

The local authorities who commissioned the work were very clear about their requirements: the building was to bring prestige to the neighborhood with a design that was ahead of its time while eschewing an elitist appearance that might inhibit users: the public should be able to identify with the building. The goal was also to create a flexible facility, adaptable to the needs of future generations.

The library designed by the architects Alsop & Stormer takes the shape of an inverted "L", with a horizontal block raised twelve meters above street level and supported partially on columns and partially on a vertical block. This design creates a covered space for outdoor activities. In addition, the cantilevered volume shades the south façade, such that neither blinds nor any other sort of sun protection were needed. Enormous stainless-steel lettering two meters tall contributes to the building's peculiar silhouette.

The horizontal block consists of a double-height space that houses the main desk, the book area and, at the north, the children's library. Three ovoid volumes on columns that house a center for Afro-Caribbean literature, a children's activities area and a conference hall inhabit this large area. Capping the largest space is a large orange skylight-roof that can be seen from the street.

The main façade is covered by metal mesh, while the south, east and west enclosures are clad in copper panels. The windows of the vertical block are of colored glass fixed with silicone to aluminium frames, forming a peculiar curtain wall.

The library was designed to take advantage of natural energy sources and thus minimize fuel consumption. Thanks to wise environmental advisement, the project gets the most out of sunlight and ventilation, making it a truly ecological building.

The library is part of an urban regeneration program for the Peckham area.

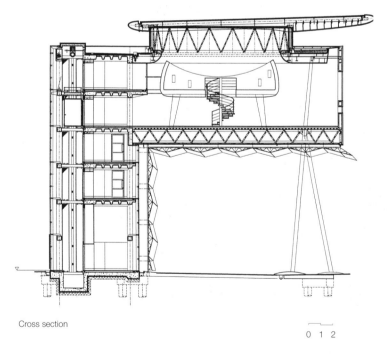

Cross section

0 1 2

The large reading room occupies the two upper levels in a double-height space lit with large windows and skylights. The aim was to minimise energy consumption, and thus natural light was exploited as far as possible: electric lighting is used only after sundown and at very localised points.

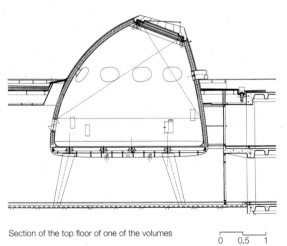

Section of the top floor of one of the volumes

0   0,5   1

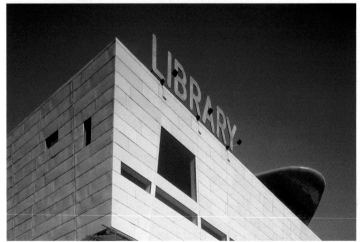

The three volumes seem to invade the space, like alien objects. The intersection with the structure of the building is quite skilful and at the ceiling generates several skylights. These bodies are clad in aircraft ply, while the interior walls are finished in plaster.

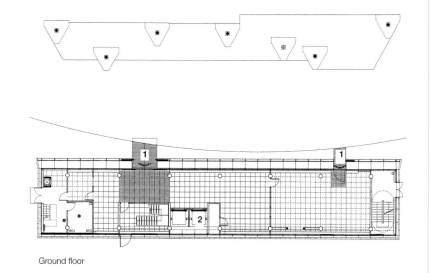

Ground floor

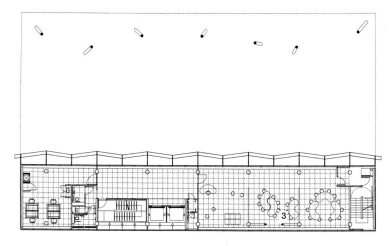

Second floor

1. Entrance
2. Elevators
3. Conference hall
4. Books
5. Reading room
6. Afro-Caribbean literature section
7. Children's library

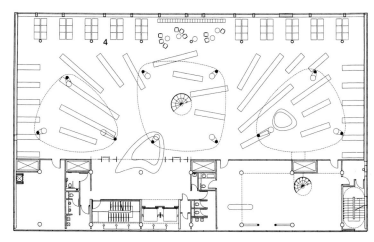

Fourth floor

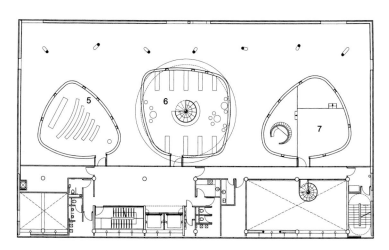

Fifth floor

0 1 2

Architects: Alsop & Stormer
Collaborators: Adams Kara Taylor
(structures), Concord Lighting Design
(lighting), Battle McCarthy (environmental
engineering).
Built: 1999
Location: London, United Kingdom
Photography: Roderick Coyne
Photograph on page 24: Klaus Frahn/Artur

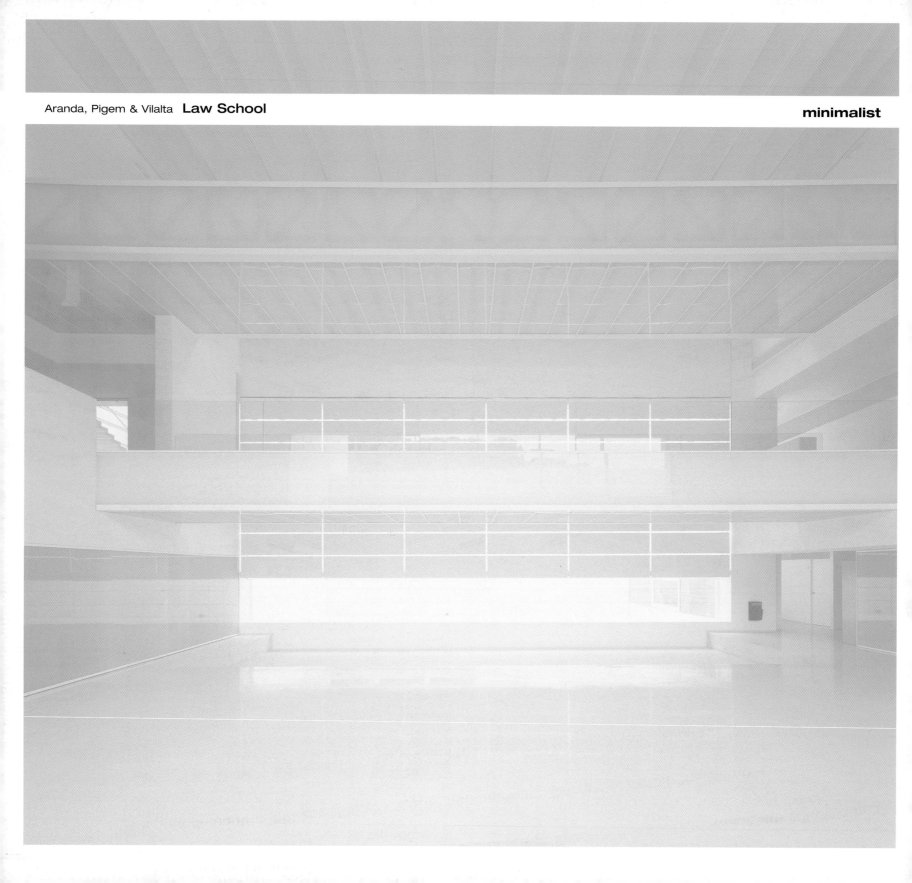

Aranda, Pigem & Vilalta **Law School**

minimalist

Vocational Training Center

The Vocational Training Center is a complex designed to accommodate young people from different countries, and includes dormitories, teaching facilities and a recreation area. The primary objective of the commission was to create a dynamic and varied environment that at the same time would make the temporary residents feel at home. It was decided to eschew monumentality in the buildings, instead opting for a project that would fit in with the landscape, with low buildings scattered around the valley in which the site lies, and abundant vegetation.

A network of tree-lined paths and trails links the town, to the south of the site, with the recreational facilities at the north. The teaching units and workshops are located near the edge of town and are arrayed around an expansive green yard. The rigid distribution of the rooms reflects a strict functional organization and a desire for all the spaces to offer views of the yard or countryside. Pitched roofs and wide eaves afford an ample variety of covered outdoor walkways and entries.

By playing with the elevations and planting trees, the architects were able to soften the impact of the complex on the area. The buildings that house the classrooms and the study areas appear to have two floors when seen from the town , while the façade that looks on to the valley reveals that they have three. The ground floor was erected in stone and the upper floors are clad in different-colored panels, creating an eclectic composition culminating in metal roofs.

The dormitories occupy a series of buildings which, embedded in the slope of the site, snake their way downhill. Thanks to their location on a greenbelt, the dormitories benefit from a double orientation: the views to the north and the light from the southeast. Most of these buildings have two upper floors and an open ground floor that provides manifold entryways for the users. Vegetation was planted on the roofs so that from afar the buildings blend in with their natural surroundings. The façades were designed in white-painted plaster and with a system of wooden projections that hold a great variety of plants. The large spans of glass allow plentiful natural light inside.

The different strategies used to dilute the impact of the work on the environment create an ensemble that appears heterogeneous only when seen from inside.

A network of tree-lined trails and paths links together all the areas of the complex.

Floor plan of the teaching units

Floor plan of the residential complex

0 4 8

Architects: Behnisch & Partner

Collaborators: Stötzer & Neher (landscape),

Christian Kandzia (color's studys)

Built: 2002

Location: Bitburg, Germany

Gross floor area: 296,236 sq. ft.

Photography: Christian Kandzia

Photograph on page 36: Eugeni Pons

Riegle Riewe **Technical University in Graz**

minimalist

Expansion of the Architecture School

The commission was based on the requirements of the Universidad Técnica Federico Santa María for the expansion of the architecture school. In the first place, the project had to redefine the functional and spatial design of the expansion of the existing building. Moreover, a period of only ten months was allowed from the initial sketches to the opening of the school, leaving three months for the design, one for calculating costs and awarding the building work, and six for the actual construction. A further restriction was the limited budget for a 19,300 sq. ft. building. Finally, emphasis was placed on the relationship with the existing buildings, both at the structural level—given that this is an area of high seismic risk—and at the formal level, by which the result would have to respect the other buildings on the campus, all in neo-gothic style and catalogued by the United Nations.

Once the requirements had been met, the architects' primary objective was to create a flexible space capable of evolving with the unpredictable design changes to which architecture schools are subject. To accommodate variable functions and future renovations, they proposed a building to a certain extent unfinished: a space which acts as an infrastructure for varied events rather than as a volume for fixed activities.

The use of cutting-edge computer design aided enormously in generating a space capable of accommodating a variety of uses. The virtual sequences served to move beyond the classic institutional typologies.

In the first stage of the work a ramp was erected leading to a large multifunctional space that can serve as an exhibition gallery, as a computer room, as an events hall or simply as an area for walking about. The second stage will add an exterior auditorium for 250 people on the roof.

The choice of materials was governed by environmental awareness and by the intention to create varied visual effects. The integration of this work with the existing buildings is achieved through the use of wavy perforated aluminum, a glass curtain wall and translucent polycarbonate panels. In addition, the façade system permits control of the light entering the interior and minimizes the transmission of heat during the hot summer months. Meanwhile, the suspended ramp acts as a blind.

The relationship between the existing buildings and the new expansion is interesting in its ingenious use of contrasts.

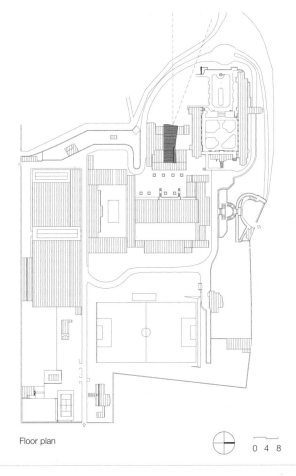

Floor plan

0 4 8

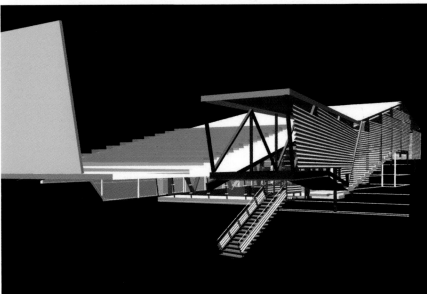

The trussed structural
system for the roof
stands out boldly in the
interior. The flooring
reflects the inclined
columns, emphasizing
the presence of the load-
bearing elements.

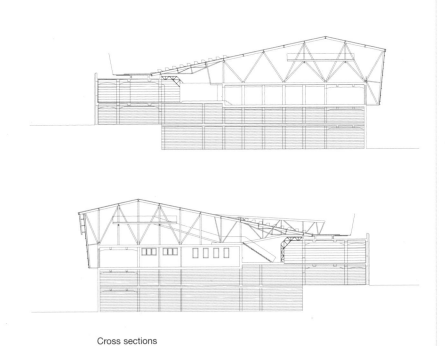

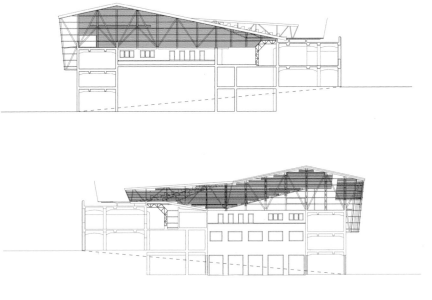

Cross sections

0 1 2

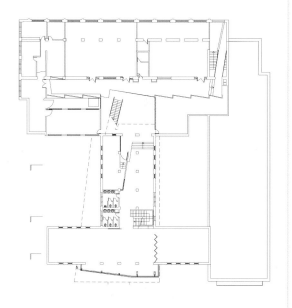

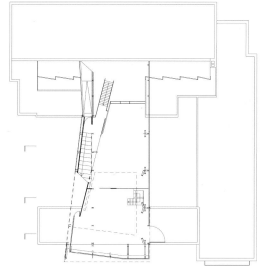

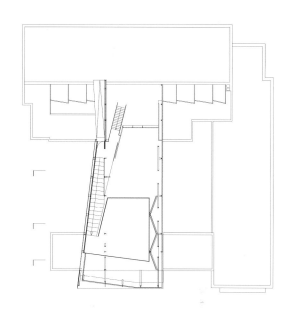

First floor

Second floor

Third floor

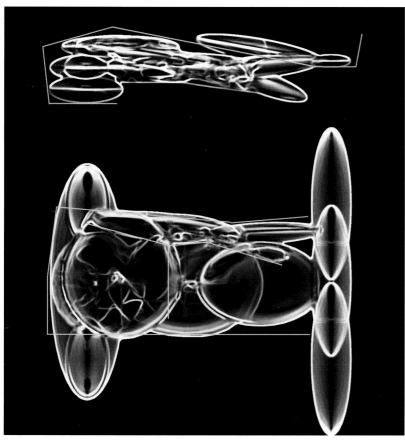

Conceptual development of the block

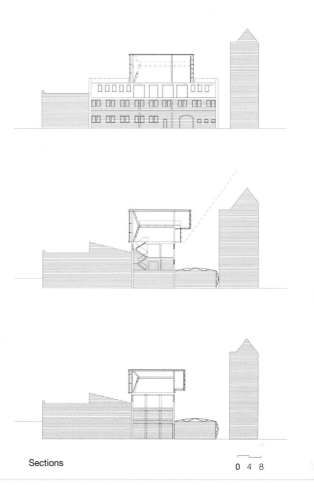

Sections

0 4 8

Architects: LWPAC, Lang Wilson Practice in Architecture Culture

Collaborators: Roberto Barria, Pol Taylor, Ricardo Luna SA (structures), Mainos SA (contractor) and Oscar Jalil (technical supervisor).

Built: 1999

Location: Valparaíso, Chile

Gross floor area: 19,300 sq. ft.

Photography: Guy Winborne

Photograph on page 42: Paul Ott

Paul de Ruiter **Mercator**

minimalist

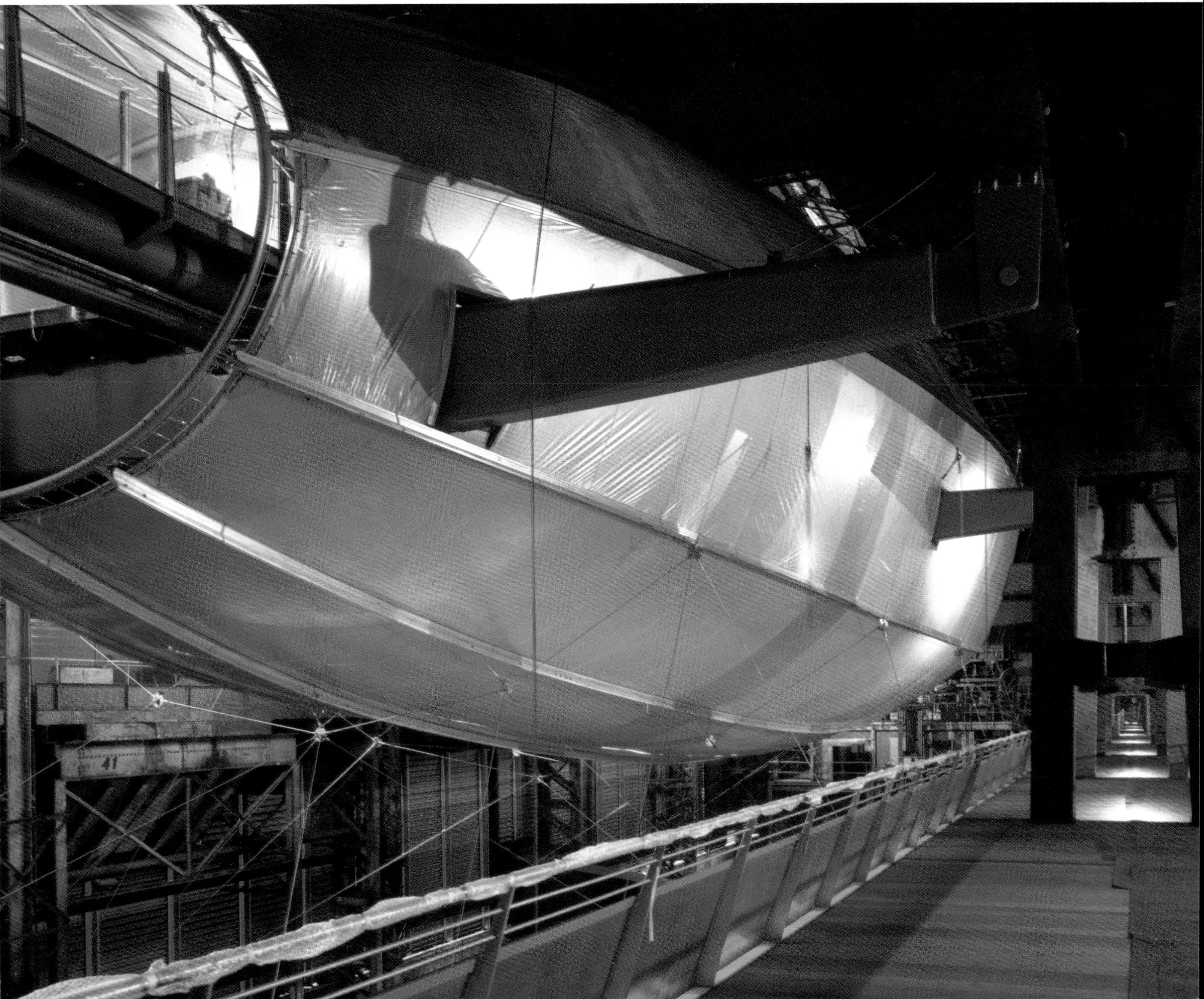
41

Magna Science Museum

The Millennium Committee is an organization that was created to promote activities during the change of millennium. Their projects in London, notably the Millennium Dome by Richard Rogers, are well known. In 1998 they commissioned Wilkinson Eyre Architects to design a new cultural facility in the small town of Templeborough, east of Liverpool. The project consisted of converting an obsolete steelworks into a science museum, the theme of which was to center on the four Aristotelian elements: land, air, fire and water. Moreover, it was to emphasize the interactivity between the visitors and the environment, and therefore from the outset sensitive and changeable construction elements were considered.

The first stage of the work was to demolish all the ancillary buildings of the foundry and repair the metal skin of the sheds, which were finally painted entirely black to unify the exterior appearance of the complex.

Four pavilions, each dedicated to one of the elements, occupy the awe-inspiring interior of the shed. The shape, location and construction process of these bodies is linked to their respective elements. In addition, retained elements associated with the steel industry make up an innovative ensemble which in turn recalls the building's original character.

The pavilions are connected by walkways and bridges which converge at the core of elevators and stairways located in the refurbished transformer building. Steel skeletons supported by the system of uprights that once sustained the crane rails comprise the structure of the new blocks.

The Air Pavilion is a giant "bubble" inflated by a sophisticated ventilation system, while a cable structure holds the pavilion in position. The Water Pavilion is clad in corrugated stainless-steel panels which form a large spiral reminiscent of water swirling down a drain. The Fire Pavilion is a three-dimensional lattice structure covered in black cladding. And the Earth Pavilion is supported by a system of columns that rise to the steel-panel roof.

The project was designed using latest-generation technology and influenced by a profound ecological awareness that led to the reuse of many of the construction elements from the old foundry.

In a single ensemble of buildings, Magna combines the past, the present and the future of construction.

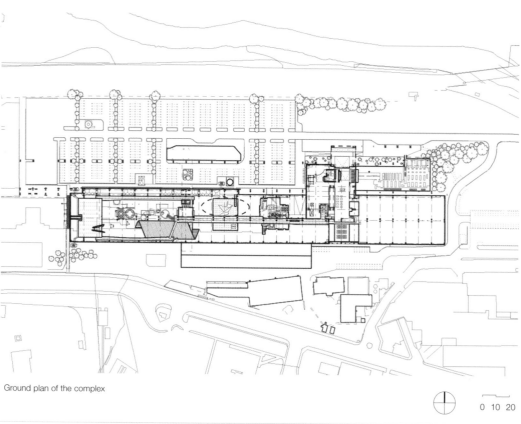

Ground plan of the complex

0 10 20

Lighting is used to generate and intensify optic effects. A good example is the lighting of the Water Pavilion, where the bluish and yellowish light of the neon lamps emphasises the sensation of movement of the metal panels.

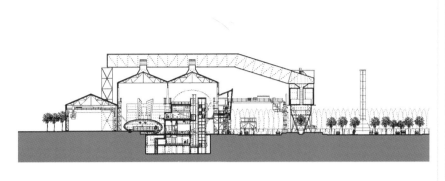

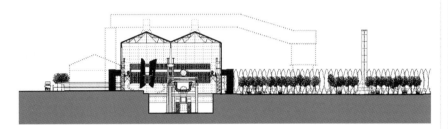

Cross sections

0 4 8

Architects: Wilkinson Eyre Architects

Collaborators: Connell Mott MacDonald (structures),

Event Communications Limited (exhibition design).

Built: 2001

Location: Templeborough, Rotherham, United Kingdom

Gross floor area: 129,000 sq. ft.

Photography: Benedict Luxmoore

Photograph on page 52: Rien van Rithoven

KHR AS **Bang & Olufsen Offices**   **minimalist**

Banco Hypo Alpe Adria

The design for the new Hypo Alpe Adria Bank headquarters, developed over three stages, had to accommodate firstly the company's head offices and a convention center, then commercial spaces and underground parking, and finally residences and a day-care center.

The site is located about 3,1 miles from the centre of the town of Klagenfurt, Austria, in an area where the urban fabric melds with farmland. The nearby constructions consist of isolated buildings surrounded by parking garage, a situation that is aggravated by the flat blocks that dot the poor, fragmented suburban landscape.

Morphosis's goal was to improve the conditions in these areas, thus they focused on integrating rural qualities with urban typologies: they designed a large vaulted roof which imitates the undulating contours of the landscape. While the pedestrian spaces were created by making incisions in this large constructed mass, the parking garage was relegated to the underground levels. The planning located the denser part of the project to the south, near the busier street, while the residential area is at the north, mixing with the suburban environment.

Users enter the complex under a large projecting roof which leads to a plaza. This space, reminiscent of a Roman forum, provides access to the banking institution, to the convention center and to an indoor network of pedestrian walkways. The offices, which face on to the street, occupy a five-storey building which seems to emerge from a collision between the mass of the building and the site. The different departments are arrayed around a sunlit courtyard. The elevators were located in the atrium, with projecting walkways that connect with the floors.

In building the complex a number of materials were employed: glass, metal and perforated aluminum panels for the façades, and concrete for the structure. Inside, terrazzo and ceramic tiles and carpeting were used for the floor, plaster for the partition walls, and wood panelling in the convention center.

The north side of the site is more spacious, with plenty of light and air and numerous gardens leading to the adjoining fields. The residential buildings and school are scattered about, adapted to the characteristics of the environs.

The building combines materials and geometries which highlight, and at the same time respect, a rural environment.

The lighting of the transitory spaces —stairways, ramps, lobby and walkways— was achieved with skylights and with glass panels on the façades. To avoid a glare a system of metal panels was installed to check the sunlight.

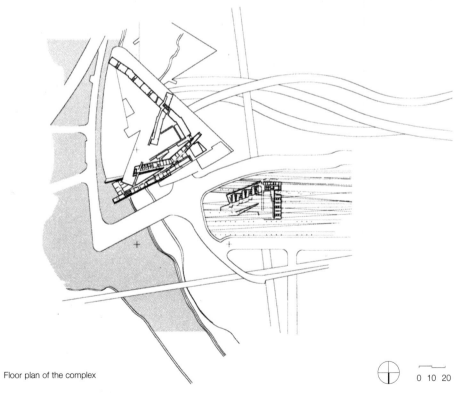

Floor plan of the complex

0 10 20

Despite the scale of the project, Morphosis proved successful in defining all the spaces with a nearly poetic composition. The penetration of natural light, the finishes and the geometric ruptures create singular spaces characteristic of these architects.

Architects: Morphosis

Collaborators: Dipl. Ing. Klaus Gelbmann, Richard Kuglitsch (structures), Robert Sorz Fritz Aufschlager (mechanical engineering).

Built: 2001

Location: Klagenfurt, Austria

Gross floor area: 1,156,193 sq. ft.

Photography: Ferdinand Neumüller and Ernst Peter Prokop

Photograph on page 58: Ib Sørensensen

Rafael Moneo **Kursaal**

minimalist

Café Musiques

Designed by the Périphériques studio and the office of Jacob & MacFarlane, the Café Musiques leisure center is located on a site straddling the frontier between a developed suburban area and countryside. To the north, the site borders on a highway, a parking garage and a business complex laid out in a scattered pattern typical of city outskirts. To the south, as far as the eye can see, there are fields, with a leafy poplar wood separating the railway line from a lake. With rushes and the water lilies this is also the ideal habitat for a great variety of birds.

The project comprises three parts differentiated both functionally and formally: the concert hall, restaurant, and entrance and transitory area. All were designed individually by different teams and, using computer technology, the designs were subsequently fused to evaluate their joining, refine the construction details of the intersections and mitigate the impact of the complex on so singular an environment.

The north façade encloses the entrance, corridors and waiting rooms, and is composed of a system of transparent and translucent colored glass. The lobby stands out for its double height and provides access to the restaurant and concert hall. With its wholly glassed-in south-facing façade, it offers magnificent views of the garden.

The concert hall is a large, totally soundproofed space eight meters in height with a barely elevated bar and a stage at opposite ends. The floor is concrete and the interior walls are galvanized metal panels. The exterior is clad with polished stainless steel panels which reflect the landscape and lessen the impact of the building.

The restaurant has a rectangular floor plan and entrances from the lobby and outside across a spacious patio. The concrete of the interior contrasts with a red-painted perforated wood ceiling. The volume containing the restaurant is clad in concrete panels into which move camouflage-like designs. On the first floor, which covers only the kitchen and part of the dining room, is a hip-hop discotheque.

The objective was to erect a building that would blend in with both urban and rural environs.

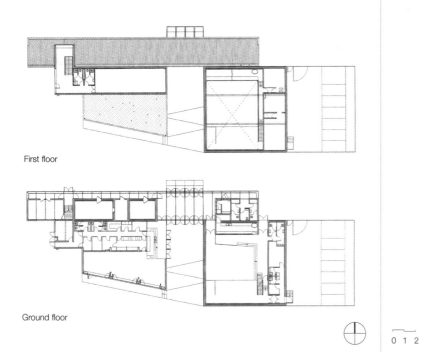

First floor

Ground floor

0 1 2

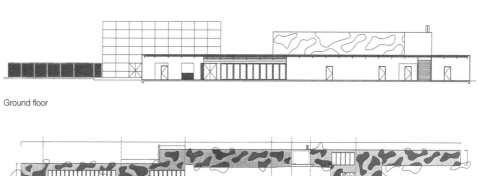

Ground floor

Sketch of the design of the concrete façade

0 1 2

Architects: Périphériques (Paillard & Jumeau +
Marin & Trottin) e Jakob & MacFarlane Architectes Associés
Collaborators: B. Douliery
Built: 1999
Location: Savigny-Le-Temple, France
Gross floor area: 12,903 sq. ft.
Photography: Luc Boegly/Archipress and N. Borel
Photograph on page 66: David Cardelús

Architects Woods Marsh **Aurora Place**

minimalist

Spa Bad Elster

The Spa Bad Elster is one of the oldest peat moss spas in Germany. Through the years it has undergone numerous modifications to improve and enlarge its installations, and thus reflects diverse architectural styles. After winning the competition for the new work, the Behnisch & Partner studio faced the challenge of restructuring the complex, including the demolition of a number of obsolete buildings, the construction of a new bathhouse and an information center, as well as the rearrangement of the existing spaces.

The original buildings are grouped around a large rectangular courtyard, on to which face in a somewhat helter-skelter manner the rear façades. The main façades, of which some in baroque style stand out, open outwards, with views of the town and the nearby woodlands. The architects' primary objective was to instill the complex with a new life: redesigning the central area and attempting to harmonize the new buildings with the existing ones.

With this project, the courtyard, formerly used as a storage area and to prepare the mud, became the heart of the complex, with the new bathhouse as its most outstanding structure. The design of the bathhouse was governed by extreme sensitivity: it was endowed with a peaceful and gratifying atmosphere which, along with its therapeutic virtues, make the building an ideal place to relax.

To strengthen the link between the interior of the bathhouse and the outdoor environment (woods and sky) and to avoid a hemmed-in feeling in the courtyard, transparent materials were chosen for all the enclosures. The façades and the roof consist of double-glazed glass, with a one-meter airspace between the layers. The exterior panels are highly insulating, while an efficient ventilation system was installed between the two layers to economize on energy, avoid condensation and create a comfortable indoor environment year round. In addition small units were installed to take advantage of the heat generated in the airspace to heat the complex in winter.

The construction system for the roof includes colored-glass louvers that offer protection from the sun and prevent glare. Since they are adjustable, in summer they can be set perpendicularly to provide shade.

The design of the bathhouse was governed by innovative construction technologies and profound ecological awareness.

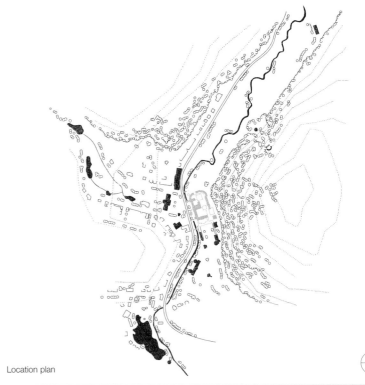

Location plan

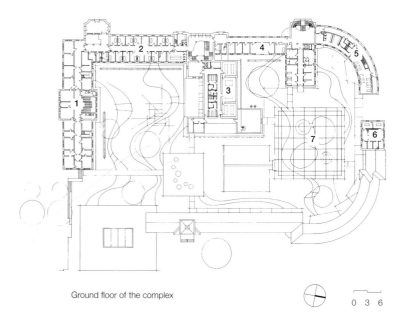

Ground floor of the complex

0 3 6

1. Offices
2. Mineral water
   treatments
3. Aerobic
4. Electric therapy
5. Sauna
6. Solarium
7. Pools

For safety reasons, the glass of the façades was laminated with a layer of polyvinyl, thus preventing flying shards of glass in the event of breakage. In addition, should any of the panels suffer damage, this type of protection ensures that the ventilation will continue to function correctly.

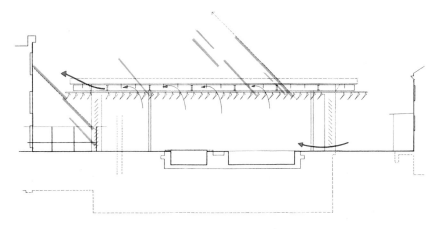

Ventilation scheme for summer

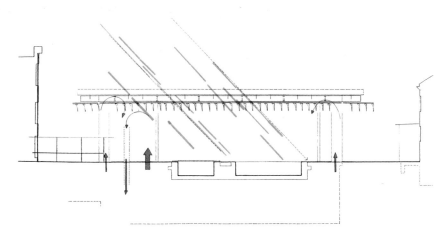

Ventilation scheme for winter

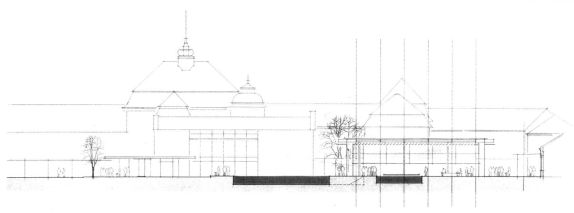

Longitudinal section

0 1 2

Architects: Behnisch & Partner

Collaborators: Luz & Partner (landscaping), Erich Wiesner (color study)

Built: 1999

Location: Bad Elster, Germany

Gross floor area: 186,236 sq. ft.

Photography: Christian Kandzia & Martin Schodder

Photograph on page 72: Shania Shegedyn

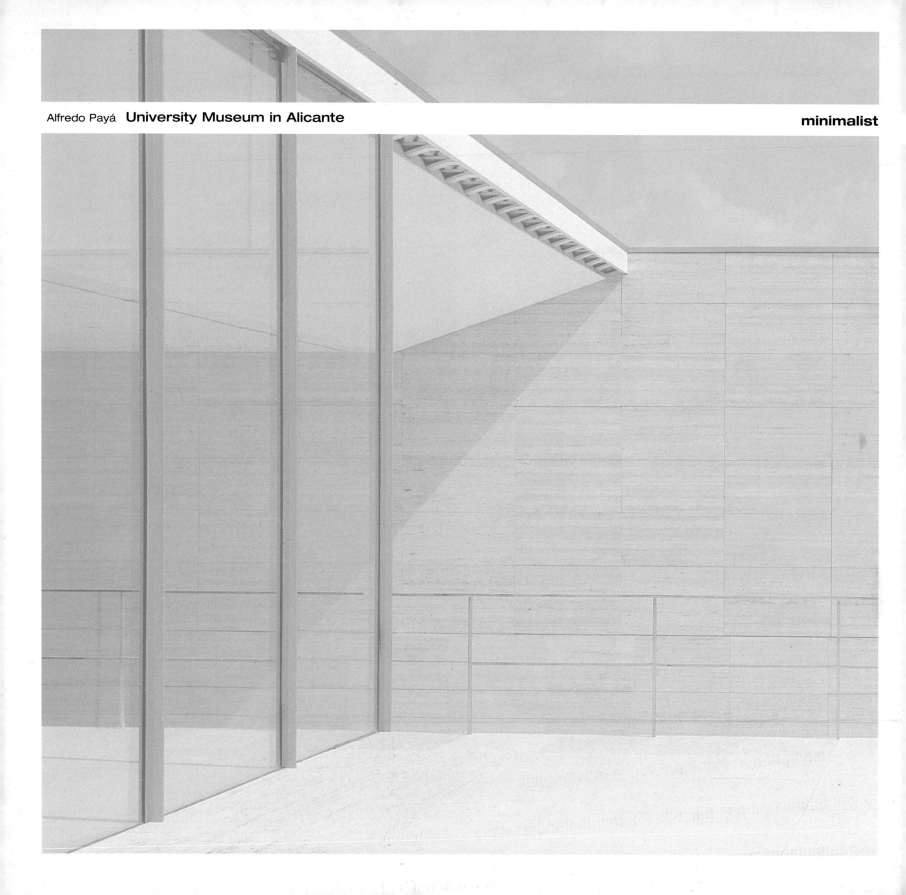

Alfredo Payá **University Museum in Alicante**

minimalist

Mind Zone

The Mind Zone is one of the fourteen individual exhibition spaces in the Millennium Dome complex. Sited on a peninsula on the Thames River east of London, the Dome is a tensed circular fabric 1,200 ft. in diameter covering a large floor area organized around a central "wheel" for exhibits and a ring for circulation. The fourteen thematic exhibition areas were given names such as Body, Play, Work, and so on. The team led by Zaha Hadid won the competition to design two of these areas, called the Mind Zone.

For this commission, the architects proposed working simultaneously with the contents of the exhibition and its structure as a single concept. This approach to the project gave rise to a work in which form and function are totally integrated.

The problem posed was how to represent the mind without resorting to its physical manifestation. The project was developed on the basis of the differentiation between the brain and the complex mechanisms of the mind it houses, such that the pavilion—configured as a succession of continuous, overlapping areas—would be the vital organ: its material presence refers to the abstraction of the mental processes, striking to the visitor's eye and inviting one to come to one's own conclusions. This design strategy eschewed excessive pedantry, instead seeking to encourage thought in the observer.

A number of artists (among them Richard Deacon and Ron Mueck) collaborated in the study of the design of the contents, which juxtapose evocation and explanation along an up-and-down route.

The singularity of the content was to have its correspondence in the materials employed in the construction of the container: fiberglass panels, lightweight and translucent, over a castellated aluminium framework, capping the steel structure and reinforcing the sensation of spatial continuity. In addition, this permitted visual communication between the different atmospheres and reflected the ephemeral character of an exhibition that was to last only a year.

The result was the creation of a space for exploring the limits at which the abstract could be attained only through the tangible.

The project sought to materialize the abstract realm of the mind, thoughts and chemical impulses.

Computer simulations allowed Zaha Hadid's studio to work with abstractions of the project, a strategy that would help generate evocative forms of the abstractions effected by the brain. These schemes also give an idea of the formal complexity of the result, where materials overlap and functions mix.

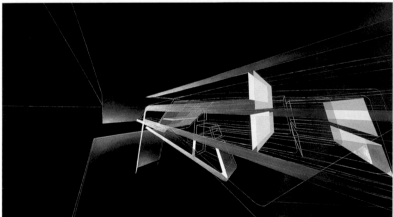

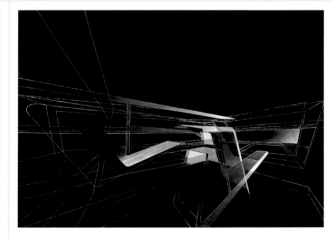

Fiberglass panels can be cut to size and in any direction, thus they can generate complex geometries and even curved shapes. Their translucence allows the movement of the users around the pavilion and the compositive elements inside to be seen from outside.

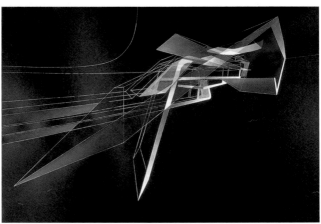

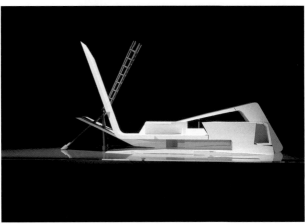

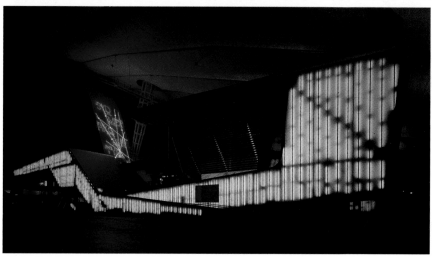

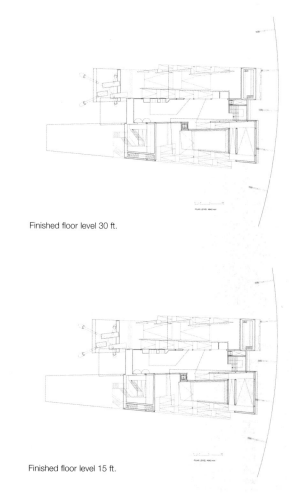

Finished floor level 30 ft.

Finished floor level 15 ft.

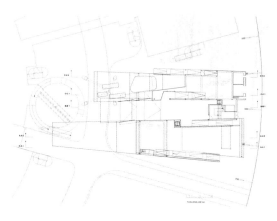

0 1 2

Finished floor level 2 ft.

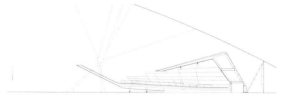

Longitudinal section

Architects: Zaha Hadid Architects

Collaborators: Ove Arup & Partners (structures), Hollands Licht (lighting).

Built: 1999

Location: Millennium Dome, London, United Kingdom

Photography: Hélène Binet

Photograph on page 58: Miguel Ángel Valero

Hiroyuki Arima + Urban Fourth **MA Gallery**   **minimalist**

MAXIMALIST

Zaha Hadid Architects **The Lounge**

The Lounge

The Kunstmuseum and the town council of Wolfsburg, Germany, commissioned Zaha Hadid to reconvert a double space and one of the lobbies in this art museum. The team headed by Hadid is also building a center dedicated to science and new technologies in the same city, so the work on this building was to anticipate the architecture of the museum complex.

At the time of construction, no specific function was assigned to two of the spaces created: a double-height gallery and a lobby on the first floor which adjoins the shop and café. Until recently, the former space had held photography exhibitions, small presentations of drawings and an educational workshop. The lobby, in the form of a balcony, served for book consulting, video screenings and as an extension of the bar.

Initially, the gallery was to house an addition to a music library belonging to the Alvar Aalto cultural center, but when the administration rejected the proposal, the space was ceded to the museum. The institution sought to become a flexible, multifunctional and dynamic center, and accordingly kept an entrance area independent from the gallery with the option of transforming it later into a space for experimentation with public functions. With a close connection to the outside environment.

Zaha Hadid's intention was thus to create a link between the gallery, the lobby and the exterior. She converted the remaining areas into a single space which accommodates different functions: it is at the same time an exhibition space for models, drawings and paintings, a gathering point for the users of the complex; a waiting room; an auditorium; a bar; a concert hall and a discotheque. The project's name, the "English voice" lounge, refers to the combination of activities for which the new area is suited: talking, relaxing, listening, drinking, sitting, dreaming and eating.

The continuity of the space was attained by covering the walls and floors in wood. The furnishings were designed by the architects themselves, who also inaugurated the space with an exhibition of selected drawings and models from their own projects.

The first exhibition in this space remodelled by Zaha Hadid was dedicated to work from her own studio.

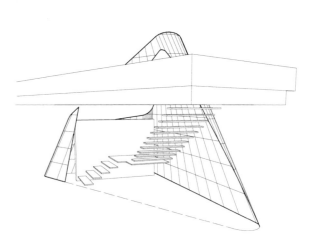

Computer-generated perspectives

Perspective of the stairway

A series of bodies of peculiar geometry occupy the two areas of the project. The volumes, generated from computer studies, have solid enclosures perforated in some cases by structural elements such as columns or beams.

The cones are irregular and cut in different directions. The resulting shapes provide display surfaces; the horizontals serve for plans and models, and the verticals for video and slide projections.

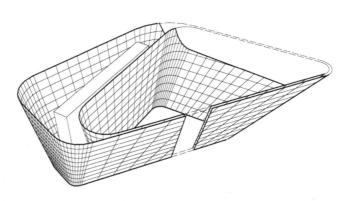

Computer study of a cone

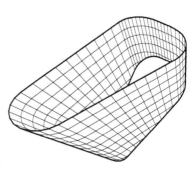

The furnishings comprise elements
of varying shapes and materials.
Their loosely defined geometry
allows the user to use them freely:
as a table, a sofa, a bed or a stool.
This flexibility also fosters endless
activities, according to the whims
of each person.

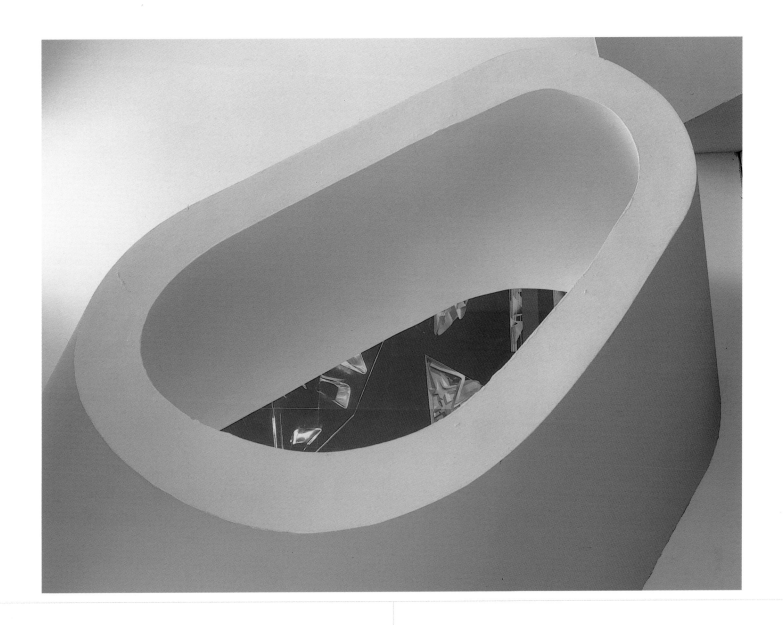

Architects: Zaha Hadid Architects

Collaborators: Woody K. T. Yao and Djordje Stojanovic

Built: 2001

Location: Wolfsburg, Germany

Gross floor area: 7,526 sq. ft.

Photography: Hélène Binet

Photograph on page 90: Koji Okamoto

MUSEUM OF ART AND TECHNOLOGY

Leeser Architecture

The formerly industrial Chelsea neighborhood in east Manhattan has become the center of New York's artistic world. Over time the most prestigious galleries have moved to this area of small garage and warehouse buildings. Amid these surroundings, the Eyebeam Atelier organization held a competition for the construction of a new museum of art and technology, won by Leeser Architecture with a complex project that blurs the traditional frontiers between production and exhibition, between the work and the viewer.

The museum was conceived as a reshapable space in which some of the floor sections can be removed and refitted quite easily. A good example of this is the forum, where the floor can be converted into a ramp, a stairway or tiered seating to suit the needs of the moment. In addition, all the surfaces that comprise the building —walls, floors and ceilings— are made of panels which conceal complete fittings with projectors, computers and other control units, and thus can be used as display supports.

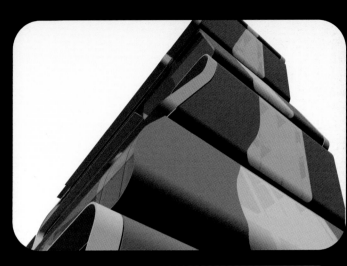

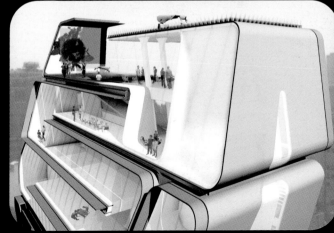

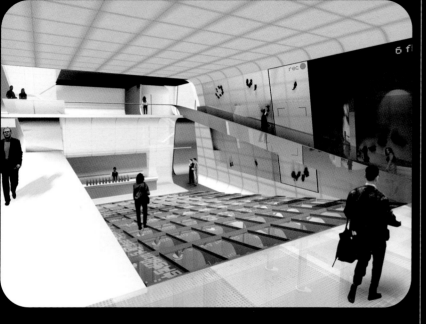

MUSEUM OF EXTREME CULTURE

LWPAC, Lang Wilson Practice in Architecture Culture

In recent years tourism has become one of the biggest industries in the world, and thus transportation, leisure, culture and tourism infrastructures have proliferated all around us and led to new urban planning projects. In this context the Museum of Extreme Culture and the Peak-to-Peak aerial cable car were conceived.

The commission received by LWPAC architects, which was to be presented in the form of an audiovisual projection, consisted of a transport station with a cable car for 180 passengers, a museum, a convention center, offices, a theater and an outdoor auditorium. All these spaces form a single, continuous and flexible landscape, capable of expanding or contracting its uses according to the season or activities program.

The architects chose light materials and prefabricated structures to facilitate and even make possible construction high up on a mountain.

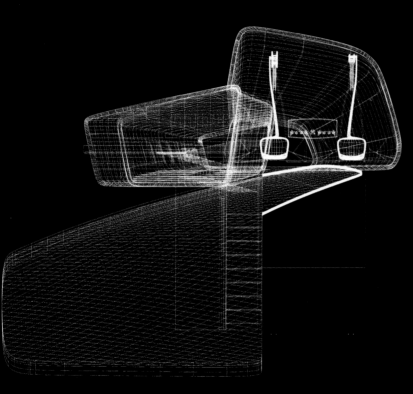

Perspective of the complex

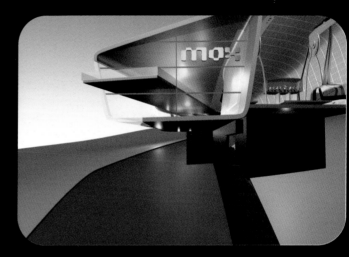

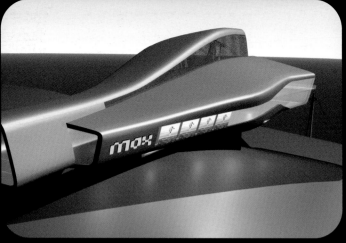

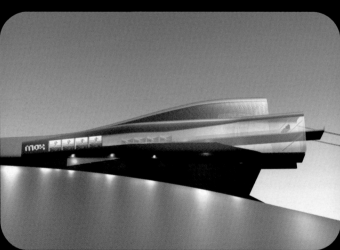

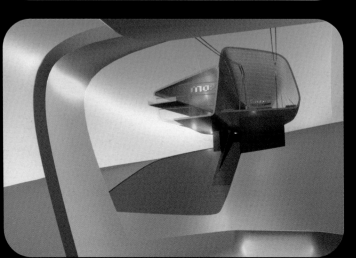

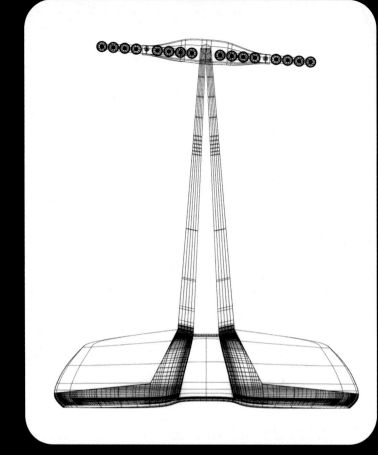

Perspective of the complex

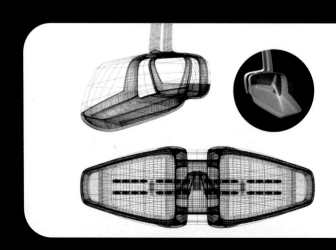

Floor plan and perspective of the cable car

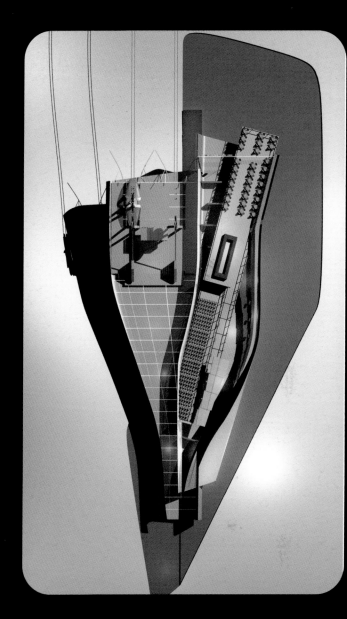

Architect: LWPAC, Lang Wilson Practice in Architecture Culture

Collaborators: Roberto E&S, Envisioning & Storytelling

Project date: 2002

Gross floor area: 19.354 sq. ft.

QUEENS MUSEUM OF ART

Eric Owen Moss Architects

The remodelling project for the Queens Museum of Art aims to bolster interaction between the public and the works on display. One of the primary goals of the work was to bring art to a greater number of people, so the new museum was oriented such that the users of the nearby highway might enjoy some of the pieces. Likewise, pedestrians in the area will be able to see part of the museum's content through its variable-opacity glass façades.

The initial work will replace the central part of the old building with a large flexible space to be used as a lobby for dance and theater performances and other activities, with tiered seating for audiences which can be converted into sloped surfaces. In addition, this spacious gallery can be enlarged by removing mobile glass panels to open it up to the adjoining spaces. From the lobby a walkway will provide the public with access to the bookshop, café and permanent exhibits.

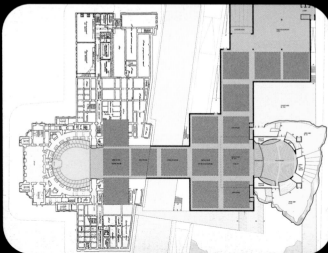

Volumetric study

Longitudinal section

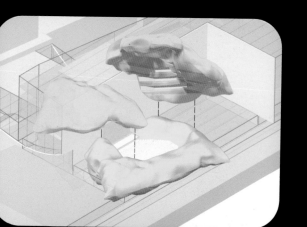

NEW HOLLAND CULTURAL CENTER

Eric Owen Moss Architects

The commission Valery Gergiev, artistic director and manager of the Mariinsky theater, awarded the Eric Owen Moss studio entails urban renewal of part of St. Petersburg, pending a study of the historical development of this area of the city. A two-pronged —cultural and ecclesiastical— renovation is planned, with the objective of stimulating economic growth and converting the city into one of the world's great cultural centers. The first will connect the area around the Winter Palace with the Mariinsky theater by means of the construction of a new complex including a luxury hotel, a museum, a new theater and office and business premises in obsolete warehouses. The second stage of the project will link up the cathedrals of St. Isaac and St. Nicholas with two walkways across a site formerly occupied by the Blagoveshinskaya church, where a new church will be built.

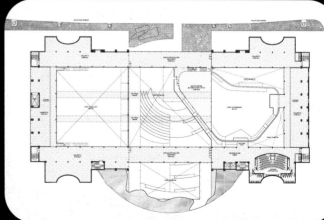

Floor plan of the complex

Boutique Christian Lacroix

Café Charbon/Nouveau Casino

Hotel Woman

Hotel Maison 140

Glass, Bot and Pod

MTV Networks Headquarters

GIORGIO ARMANI

Boutique Christian Lacroix

The Swiss studio Caps Architects, led by Christophe Carpente, was commissioned to design the new Christian Lacroix clothing shop in Tokyo. Lacroix, who had already worked with the architects on previous occasions, set out certain premises: "The project must respect the chosen setting; despite a forceful implantation of the firm's presence, the shop cannot ignore the architectural framework into which it is being introduced." From the outset Carpente sought a project which oozes temporality, which evokes the nomadism of travellers, capable of change, of adapting itself to the specific needs of each space.

The shop is distributed on two floors and enclosed within a totally transparent façade overprinted with a calligraphy text by Lacroix himself. The between-floors slab does not meet the façade, thus the enclosure appears continuous, broken up only by a subtle aluminium-work framing.

The layout of both floors is governed by the deployment of the displays. The customer's itinerary is marked out by these furnishings, which are moveable to make the shop easily transformable. The displays were conceived as transparent coloured-glass modules offering the public varied perspectives of different hues. The right angles of these furnishings contrast with the curvy chairs by the designer Pierre Paulin, as well as with the fitting rooms, shells of organic contours lined with silky, golden velvety fabrics.

The existing structure of the premises remained unchanged and only the distribution was altered, tearing out all the partitions while the preserved outer walls were painted completely white with a subtle coat of nacre. These surfaces serve for the projection of videos and photos by artists and some of the firm's habitual collaborators, such as Joël Bartolomeo, Delphine Kreuter, Nils Udo and Bernard Quesniaux. The electrical fittings were concealed in stacked metal boxes which recall those old building blocks kids used to play with. The lighting consists of spotlamps directed at the clothing and coloured furnishings.

"We wanted to go beyond simple white cubes to re-establish the balance between geometry and organics."

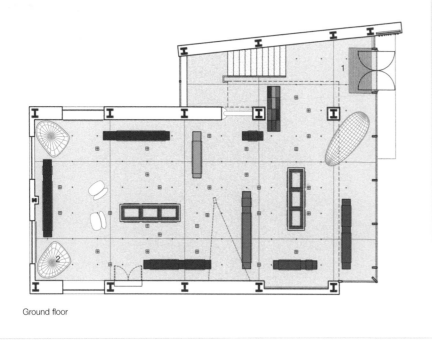

Ground floor

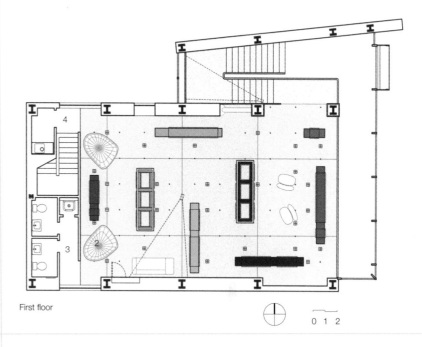

First floor

1. Entrance
2. Fitting rooms
3. Toilets
4. Storeroom

CHRISTIAN
LACROIX
PARIS

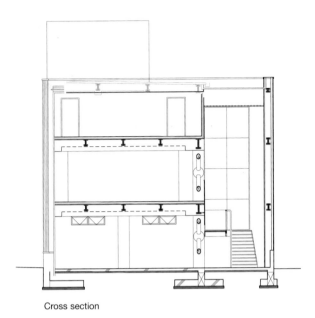

Cross section

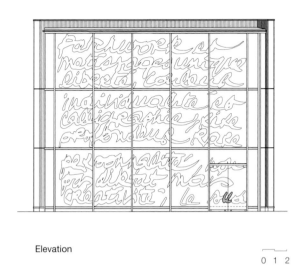

Elevation

0 1 2

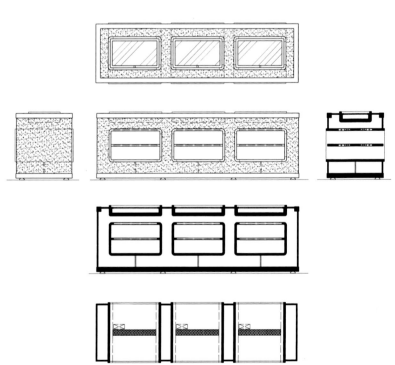

Bases, sections and elevations of the furnishings

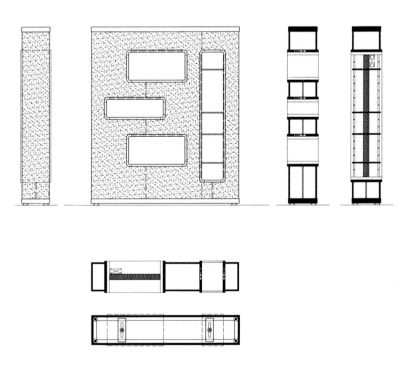

0 1 2

Architect: Caps Architects

Colaborators: Ueno Glass (furniturre production), Obayashi Construction (building), Axe design (local architects), Ansorg GmbH (light), Glace Controle (holographics films).

Built: 2001

Location: Tokyo, Japan

Gross floor area: 2,688 sq. ft.

Photography: Nácasa & Partners

Photograph on page 114: Matteo Pizza

Claudio Lazzarini & Carl Pickering **Bar Restaurant Nil**   **minimalist**

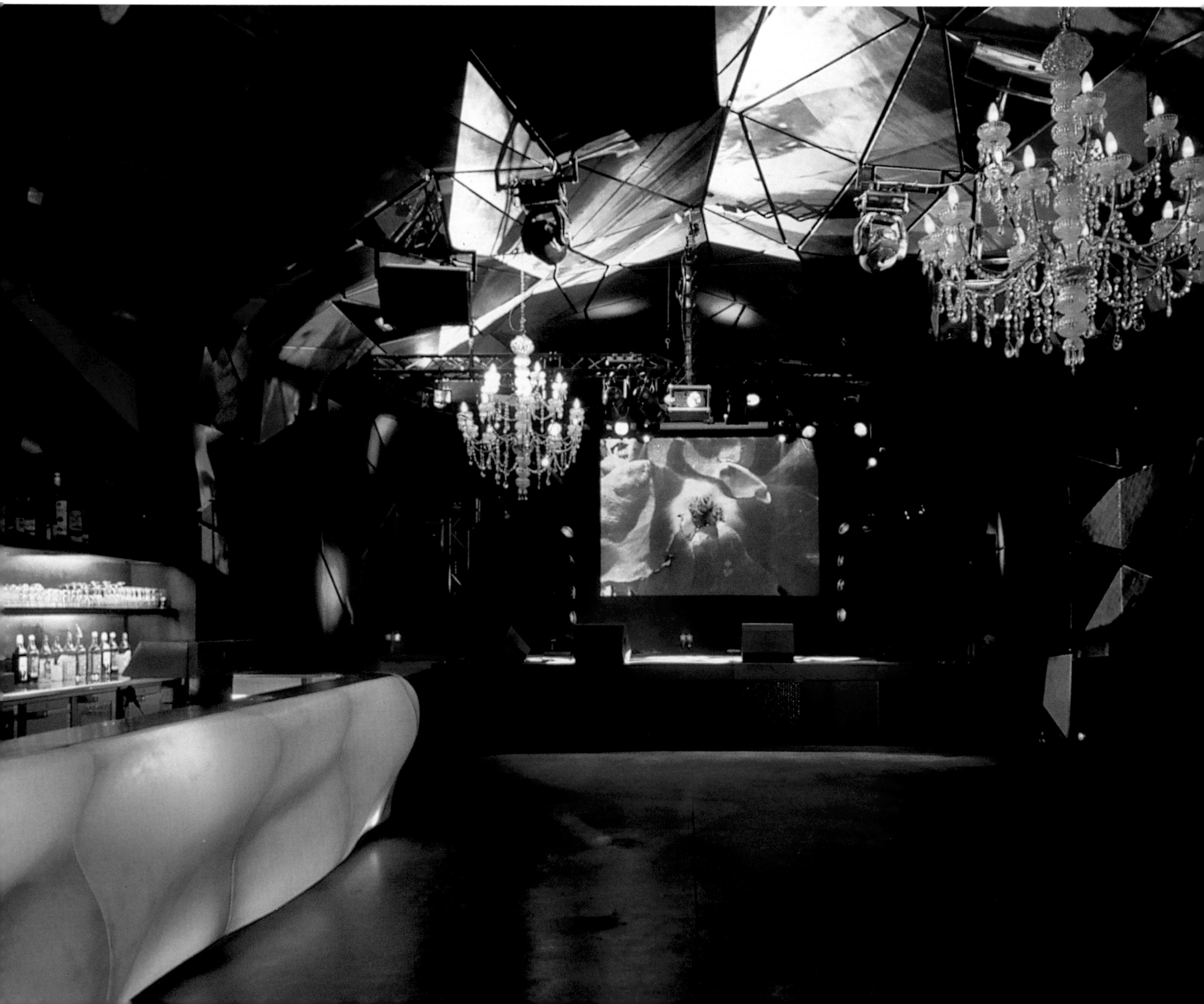

Café Charbon/Nouveau Casino

The project developed by the Périphériques group occupies the back of a beautiful early twentieth-century Parisian café, the Café Charbon. The architects' brief called for the design of a new dance club, to be called Nouveau Casino, which would include a concert hall for 300 people, a bar and a restaurant.

One of the primary objectives was to avoid interfering with the activity on the original premises, and accordingly the design included an independent entrance and a perfect soundproofing system. The entrance to the original café is through a glass façade with doors and windows that open on to the street, while access to the concert hall is through a small metal door at one end of the enclosure. A corridor runs the length of the site to the club, where it disappears in a diaphanous space with no partitions. This corridor is lit with small red spotlamps recessed in a ceiling of perforated panels.

The architects took advantage of the space's considerable height to create, at one end, a mezzanine with tables and sofas, under which are located the toilets, and, at the other end, to raise the stage and backstage storage area. The bar follows the contours of the dividing walls, leaving a large area free for dancing or simply listening to the music in comfort.

From the outset the designers' intention was to create a changing and flexible space capable of accommodating simultaneously different ambiences. Clubs are subject to the whims of fashion, and thus it is not surprising that they should fall from favor as club-goers hunger for new sensations and settings in which to interact with music. With that in mind, the architects came up with a system that allows the setting to be changed in a matter of seconds and generates an infinite range of ambiences. A system of projectors was installed to cast images on the walls and ceiling, both covered with triangular steel-plated panels arrayed in varying orientations so that they scatter the reflected light.

The projection of images on the walls and ceiling allows the ambience to be transformed in seconds.

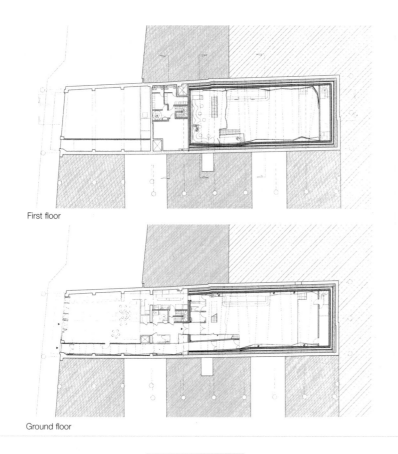

First floor

Ground floor

0 1 2

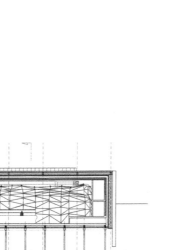

Cross section

Architects: Louis Paillard & Anne Françoise

Jumeau, of Périphériques

Collaborators: Paris Comptoirs (building),

Christophe Valtin and Shirin Raissi

(synthesis images).

Built: 2001

Location: Paris, France

Gross floor area: 5,376 sq. ft.

Photography: Luc Boegly/Archipress

Photograph on page 122: Matteo Piazza

Anouska Hempel **The Hempel**

minimalist

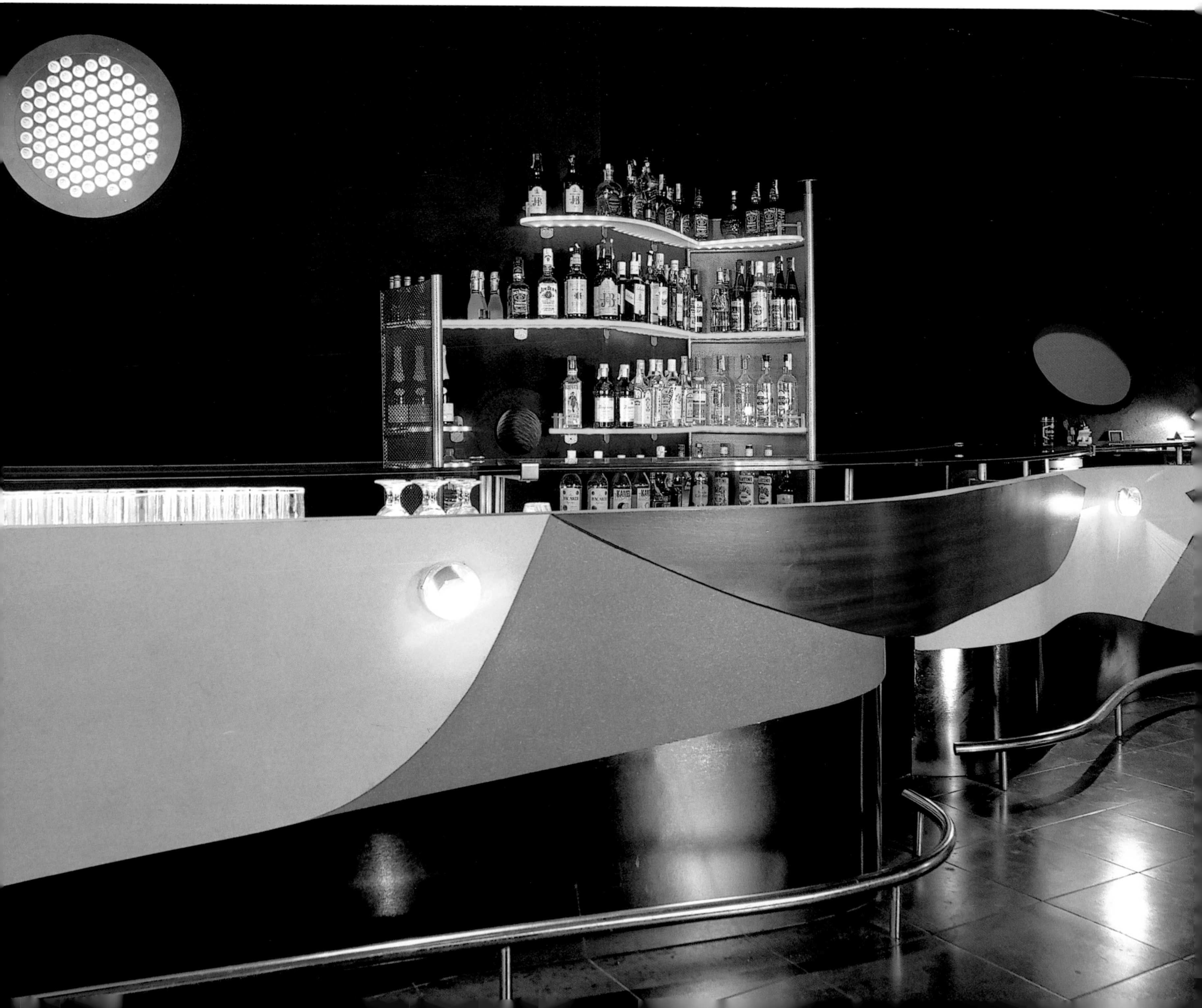

Hotel Woman

Lola Lago received the commission for the interior design of a hotel that was already partially built. The design, subject to a very restricted budget, was intended to finish a building in which the structure, part of the partitioning and even some of the fittings were already in place.

The hotel stands in an industrial area of Terrassa, a city in the Barcelona metropolitan area, and has a 2,688 sq.ft.-rectangular floor plan. The ground floor includes the bar, a dressing room, a dining room and a storage room. The guest rooms, an office and another storage room are on the first floor.

From the outset the intention was to give the hotel a festive and original air with furnishings designed by the interior designer herself. In the rooms the atmosphere was to be warm and intimate; in the bar relaxed and whimsical.

The design project sought to recreate and reinterpret twelve twentieth century decorative trends, with each bedroom given a distinctive air and named for a famous woman: for example, the Marilyn room, which was given a '50s atmosphere, or the Madonna room, decorated with aesthetic references to the '80s.

The barroom, which is not used exclusively by hotel guests, was conceived as a dark space with spot and indirect lighting. The floor, with a curved plan, is covered with black porcellanous tiling, while the plaster walls are painted black as well. The furnishings, manufactured from a range of materials encompassing plastic, metal, ceramic and fabric, are employed like sculptural elements and placed such that they create unique spaces.

The bar itself is curved and has a metal structure covered in varnished walnut. The worktop is black concrete, while the serving surface is covered in translucent safety glass, allowing a screen-printed wood veneer to show through. The bottle shelves conform to the sinuous lines of the floor plan and walls and are made of black-painted iron framework and polished transparent methacrylate shelving enclosed with small colored filters. A large projector fixed to a lightweight black-painted metal structure hangs from the ceiling.

From the furnishings to the finishings, everything was designed specially for the project.

The furnishings were designed in a broad spectrum of colors and finishes so as to stand out in a space painted entirely black. The lighting highlights these elements, affording them the leading role in the atmosphere.

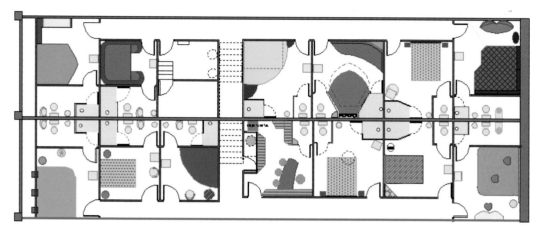

Ground floor

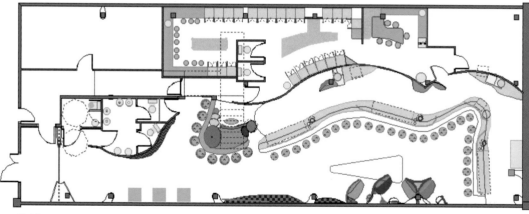

First floor

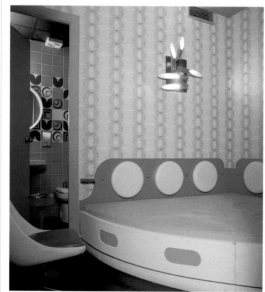

0 1 2

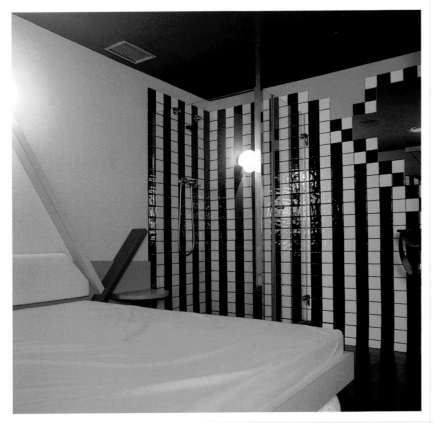

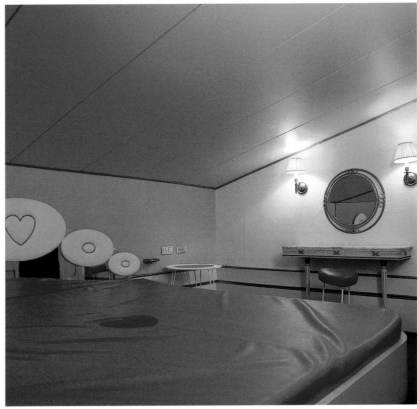

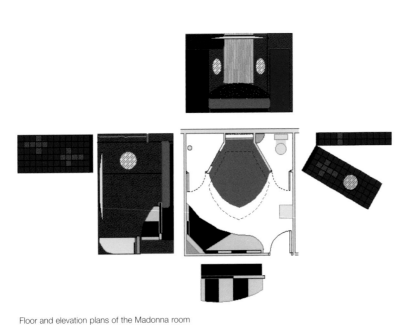

Floor and elevation plans of the Madonna room

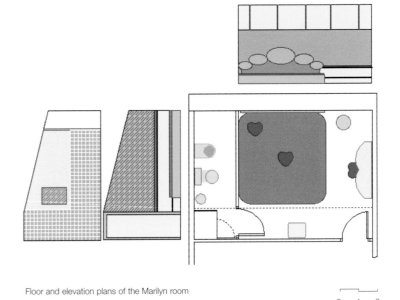

Floor and elevation plans of the Marilyn room

0 1 2

Architect: Lola Lago

Collaborators: Juan Bové, Juan Calaf and

Javier Domínguez

Built: 2001

Location: Terrassa, Barcelona, Spain

Gross floor area: 5,376 sq. ft.

Photography: Eugeni Pons

Photograph on page 128: Gunnar Knechtel

Alan Liberman **Whitelaw**   **minimalist**

Hotel Maison 140

The Maison 140 is located in the heart of Beverly Hills, between Santa Monica and Wilshire Boulevard, an area abounding in boutiques and commercial premises. The building was erected in 1930 and formerly known as the Beverly House Hotel, which the interior designer Kelly Wearstler and architects Tolkin & Associates were commissioned to renovate and transform into the new hotel.

A desire to blend styles was the guiding principle in the decoration of this California hotel. The interiors recreate styles from an exaggerated eighteenth-century French one to marked oriental references, including touches of baroque and classicism and the exoticism of other cultures —an amalgam of styles and shapes resolved with a chromatic palette in which black, red and white emerge as the leading players.

The minimalist tendency —the "less is more" idea championed by Mies van der Rohe— which currently seems to infect most vanguard scenes bypasses the door at the Maison 140, a compendium of exuberance.

The hotel opts for exaltation of excess and has taken up another, no less true motto: "Too much is never enough." Those responsible for this stylistic flight of fancy, a willful reinterpretation of bygone eras, set out to create a building situated on the opposite end of the design spectrum from so many found around the city, halfway between the history and fantasy, and charming to boot.

The rigorousness of black dominates the walls of the lobby and bar. A large panel, drawing on seventies aesthetics, composed of twelve white medallions separates the minuscule reception area from the more expansive spaces. The clarity of the panel contrasts with the dark, dense furnishings of adjacent areas like the bar, where low tables of Asian inspiration are arrayed amid turn-of-the-century pieces and acrylic-upholstered stools give it the attractive appearance of a private club.

This image is underscored by the use of lacquered panels framing Chinese mirrors with painted floral motifs and birds, crystal lamps and black chairs, elements which lend an air of luxurious decadence.

And if the bar is the ideal setting for gatherings, the 45 guest rooms are the space reserved for the fantasy. A hall, also black, leads to the rooms, behind whose doors awaits an dreamy world dominated by color.

The guest rooms are eclectically decorated with wallpaper, hangings and lacquers.

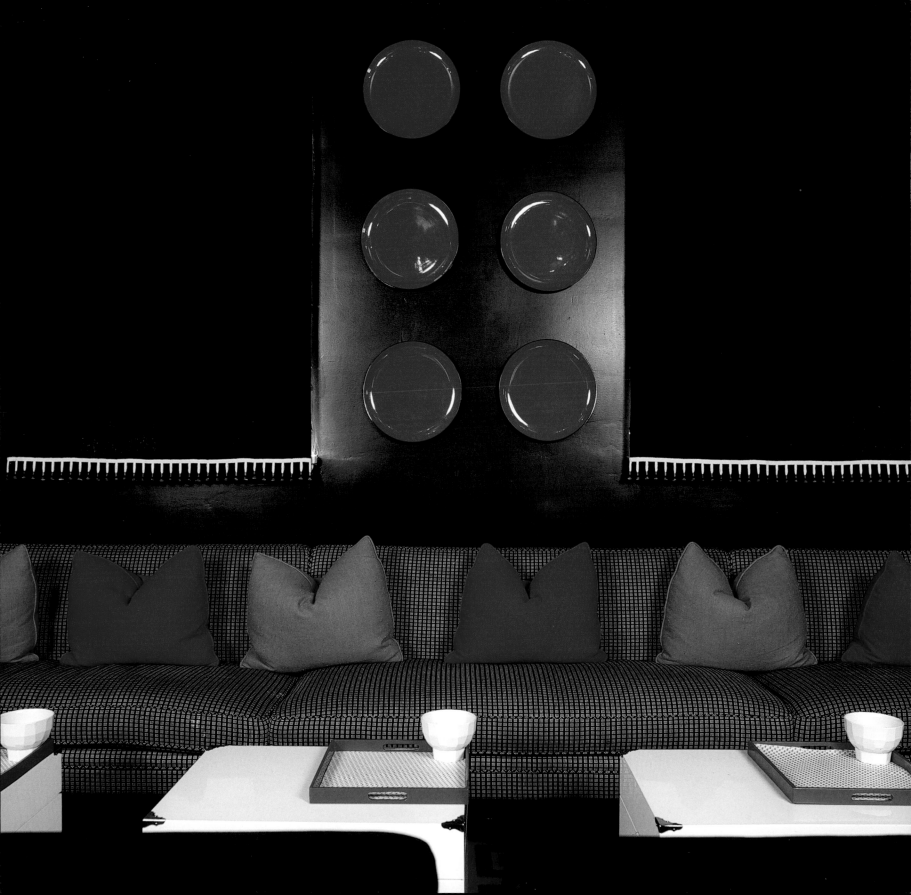

The orange main door
to Maison 140 conceals
interiors abounding in
ideas. The small
reception area features
a baroque desk, where
symmetrically-ordered
white room keys stand
out against black walls,
and opens on to
tremendously eclectic
common areas.

Architects: Tolkin & Associates

Collaborators: Kelly Wearstler Interior Design (KWID)

Built: 2000

Location: Beverly Hills, California, USA

Photography: Undine Pröhl

Photograph on page 136: Pep Escoda

Sandra Teruella & Isabel López **El Japonés**

Glass, Bot and Pod

In recent years the studio led by Thomas Leeser has designed three premises in some of New York's trendier neighborhoods: Chelsea, for example, attracting the most prestigious art galleries, or Williamsburg, home to a large artists' colony. The Glass Bar and the restaurants Bot and Pod form part of the ongoing urban renewal that these old industrial areas exemplify.

The Glass Bar, standing between garage doors and old shop windows, boasts an original façade of translucent white panels framing a blue square of glass, which also serves as the mirror in the bathroom, located just inside. Upon entering, one comes first to the toilets and then a single compact space of curvy lines tracking computer-designed contours. A single surface comprises the walls, the ceiling, benches —which appear to float in space— and, emerging from the floor, the bar. The back of the site is occupied by an enclosed patio with views of the sky and the upper floors of the neighboring factory buildings.

The Bot restaurant was also designed using computers, generating continuous shapes with straight spans joined by organically-inspired curves. Here color plays an important role, emphasizing the movement of the surfaces. The façade is composed of glass panels partially covered with light-blue plastic film. The interior is divided up by yellow partitions that contrast with the white of the furnishings. The interior garden was reserved for an outdoor dining area and covered with a white retractable awning.

The design of the restaurant Pod conceptually reproduces American suburbia: the main dining room is an abstract take on a typical bedroom-community home, with a small garden at the back, here represented by silk-screened trees on the windows. A large wide-angle photo of a trailer park further evokes the recreated landscape. This project also used computer technology to generate the enveloping shapes of the premises.

Leeser Architecture succeeded in creating three very different spaces based on similar logic and resources: a minimalist discourse fostering spaces rich in shapes and colors thanks to overwhelming imagination and the use of cutting-edge technology.

Glass, Bot and Pod combine elaborate, computer-generated geometric shapes.

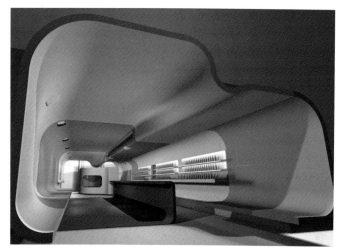

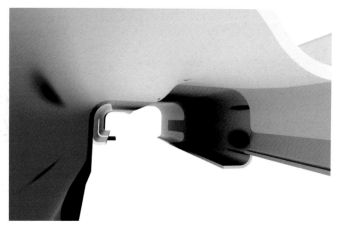

Glass Bar

Bot Restaurant

Computer-generated perspectives of the Pod Restaurant

Pod Restaurant

Architect: Leeser Architecture

Collaborators: Caroline Vanbiervliet, Marco
Bevilaqua, Max Zinnecker, Andy Saunders,
Raymond Kwok and David Riebe

Built: 2001

Location: New York, USA

Photography: Matthu Placek

Photograph on page 142: Eugeni Pons

Daniel Rowen **Osho Offices**   **minimalist**

MTV Networks Headquarters

Before embarking on the design work, the architects Felderman & Keatinge set out the goals for the new MTV Networks headquarters on the west coast of the United States. The brief required functional and comfortable, almost homelike, work spaces, distributed on five floors, each endowed with distinct aesthetics. In addition, the building had to blend in with and respect the urban environment as well as stand out as a symbol of the company, establishing a unique corporate identity capable of representing the company's philosophy. In response to all these requirements, the designers came up with an innovative architecture that reflected the client's reputation as a leader in the entertainment and communications industry.

The first efforts were invested in creating an entrance that would link the building with the sea and local vegetation. A plaza with sand-colored flooring leads into the lobby, recalling the entries of the area's traditional architecture where the dividing line between outside and inside is blurred. The façade consists of three- and five-storey metal panels forming a profile that evokes the ocean waves. An enormous boat-shaped sign announces the name of the company in rough-hewn steel lettering.

A stunning 1957 Airstream aluminium trailer greets visitors and serves as a waiting room. Inside, the decoration recreates the fifties: a pink carpet, white and black linoleum and a formica-topped kitchen table. Next to the trailer television monitors are deployed in the shape of a face, giving the sensation that the images beam out of the eyes and mouth. The lobby is also furnished with a reception desk made of a boat skeleton clad in aluminium and a copper-topped conference table.

The offices are separated by low partitions made to look like the house façades, including casement windows, wood siding, garden fences and painted-on hedges and trees. In keeping with the client's requirement that the spaces should be informal, the conference rooms were designed in living-room style, with televisions, carpets and sofas.

The work encompasses a range of finishes, furniture of different vintages and exposed fittings, creating a very heterogeneous whole.

The interior combines an austere concrete skeleton covered with sophisticated finishes and materials such as painted wood, braided wool fabrics, gauze curtains and metal panels. Glimpses of the fittings and structure can be seen among all the typical office elements and decorative details.

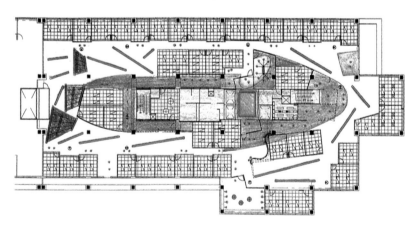

Second floor

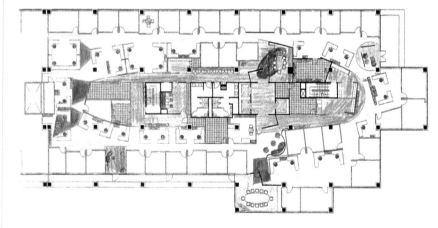

Fourth floor

0 1 2

Architects: Felderman & Keatinge Associates

Built: 1999

Location: Santa Monica, United States

Gross floor area: 110,000 sq. ft.

Photography: Toshi Yoshimi

Photography on page 148: Michael Moran

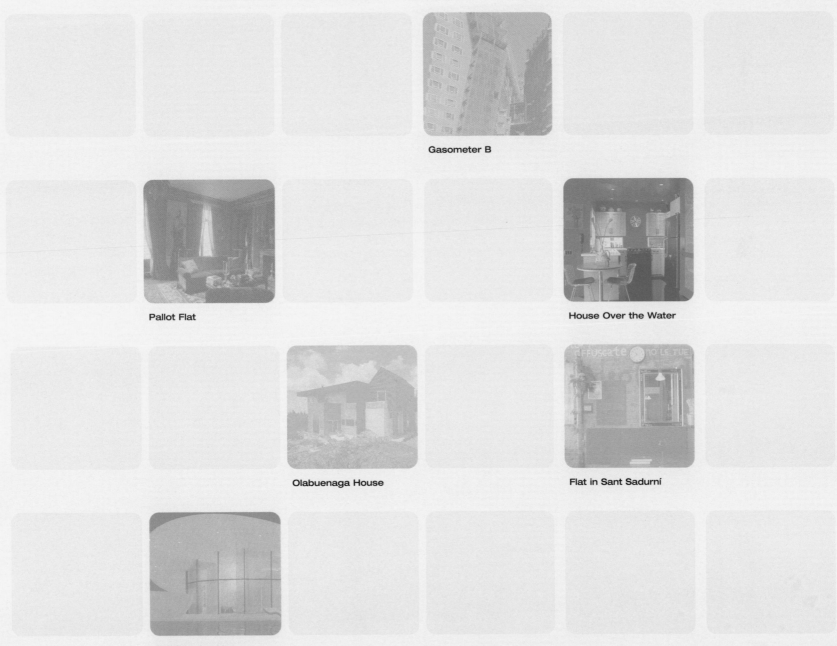

Gasometer B

Pallot Flat

House Over the Water

Olabuenaga House

Flat in Sant Sadurní

Austintonian House

Leon & Woalhage **Offices and Dwellings in Hamburg**

minimalist

Gasometer B

The four Gasometers comprise an old gas storage facility that once supplied Vienna. After being closed down the facility was demolished, with only the striking brick façades left standing. The particular location of these buildings in an industrial area, along with the unusual character of the resulting spaces, led to their being used for years as cultural centers for numerous activities.

The location of the project presented a magnificent opportunity to develop the urban fabric on the outskirts of Vienna, given that the renovation went hand-in-hand with improvements in the transport system, including the extension of a metro line and the construction of a new motorway. Apart from Coop Himmelb(l)au, three other architecture studios participated in the project, designing new housing concepts, a shopping center and a leisure complex, converting the site into a new focal point for the city.

The project developed by Coop Himmelb(l)au for Gasometer B entailed the addition of three new volumes: a large cylinder inside the Gasometer, a striking shield-shaped flat block just beside the latter, and a multifunctional space for holding different sorts of events at the base.

Flats and offices were located inside the cylinder and in the new building. A conical courtyard was designed to provide natural light for the indoor spaces of the cylinder, while north-facing balconies serve the same function for the flats in the new building. The 360 residences range in type from spacious homes with terraces to small studios for students. The combination of office and residential uses is intended to generate new ways of living and working in a single environment.

Access to the Gasometer, with different entrances for visitors and residents, is from the street or directly from the metro station. All the former Gasometers are interconnected through the shopping center, which stretches the length of the base of the complex.

The structure of the flat block is comprised of a system of concrete columns rising from foundation to roof. Glass and aluminum curtain walls enclose the flats, which thanks to their limited depth get plenty of sunlight.

The extraordinariness of the project, the provision of new residences, the creation of a shopping, leisure and cultural area, and the regeneration of this industrial district have made the Gasometers Vienna's alternative urban center.

The Gasometers constitute the focus of a new urban centre in Vienna.

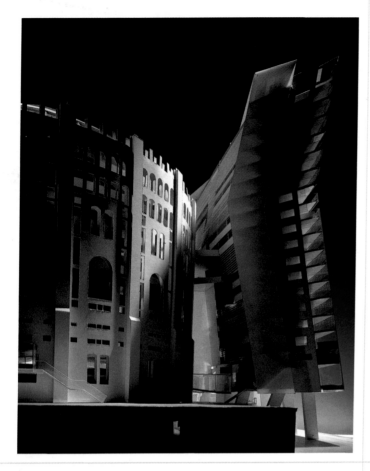

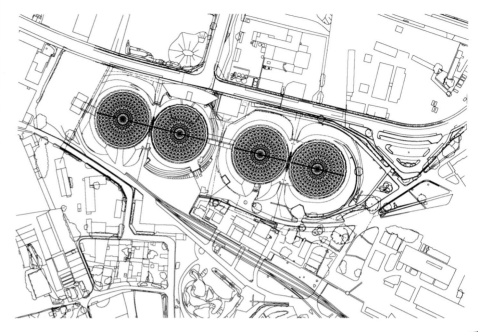

Location plan

The project developed by Coop Himmelb(l)au is notable for the skill with which they resolved the restoration of the former gas storage facility, with the forthrightness of the design of the new building, with its markedly innovative shapes. The complex is a prodigious fusion of past and future.

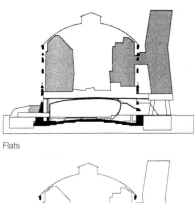

Flats

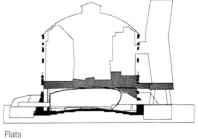

Flats

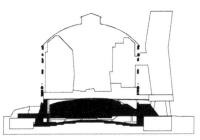

Leisure

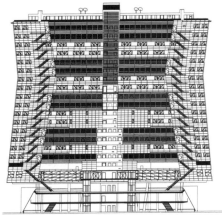

South elevations

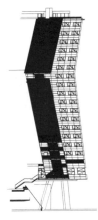

0 2 4

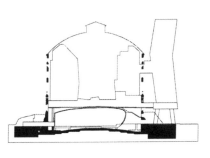

Functional scheme. Parking

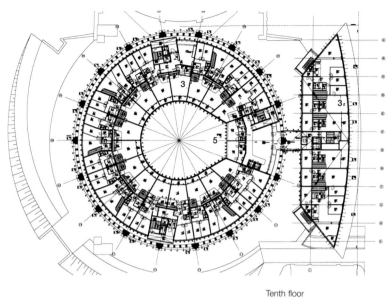

Tenth floor

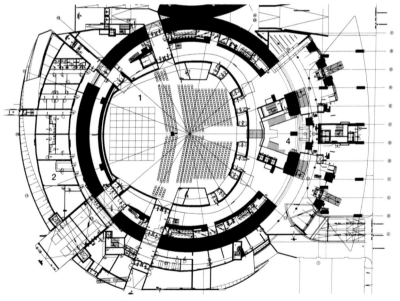

Ground floor

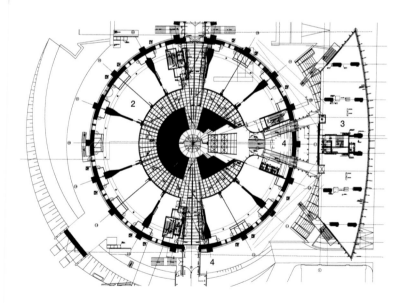

1. Auditorium
2. Offices
3. Housing
4. Entrance
5. Courtyard

Basement

0 4 8

The scale of the project required the sketching of an enormous diversity of interior spaces. Housing, offices, shopping centers, and spaces for access and communication were designed with common objectives: ecology and maximum use of natural resources, translating into warmth and comfort.

Architects: Coop Himmelb(l)au

Collaborators: Fritsch-Chiari (structures), Kress & Adams (lighting).

Built: 2000

Location: Vienna, Austria

Gross floor area: 376,344 sq. ft.

Photography: Gerald Zugmann

Photograph on page 158: Klaus Frahm

Mark Guard Architects **Dwelling on the Thames**

minimalist

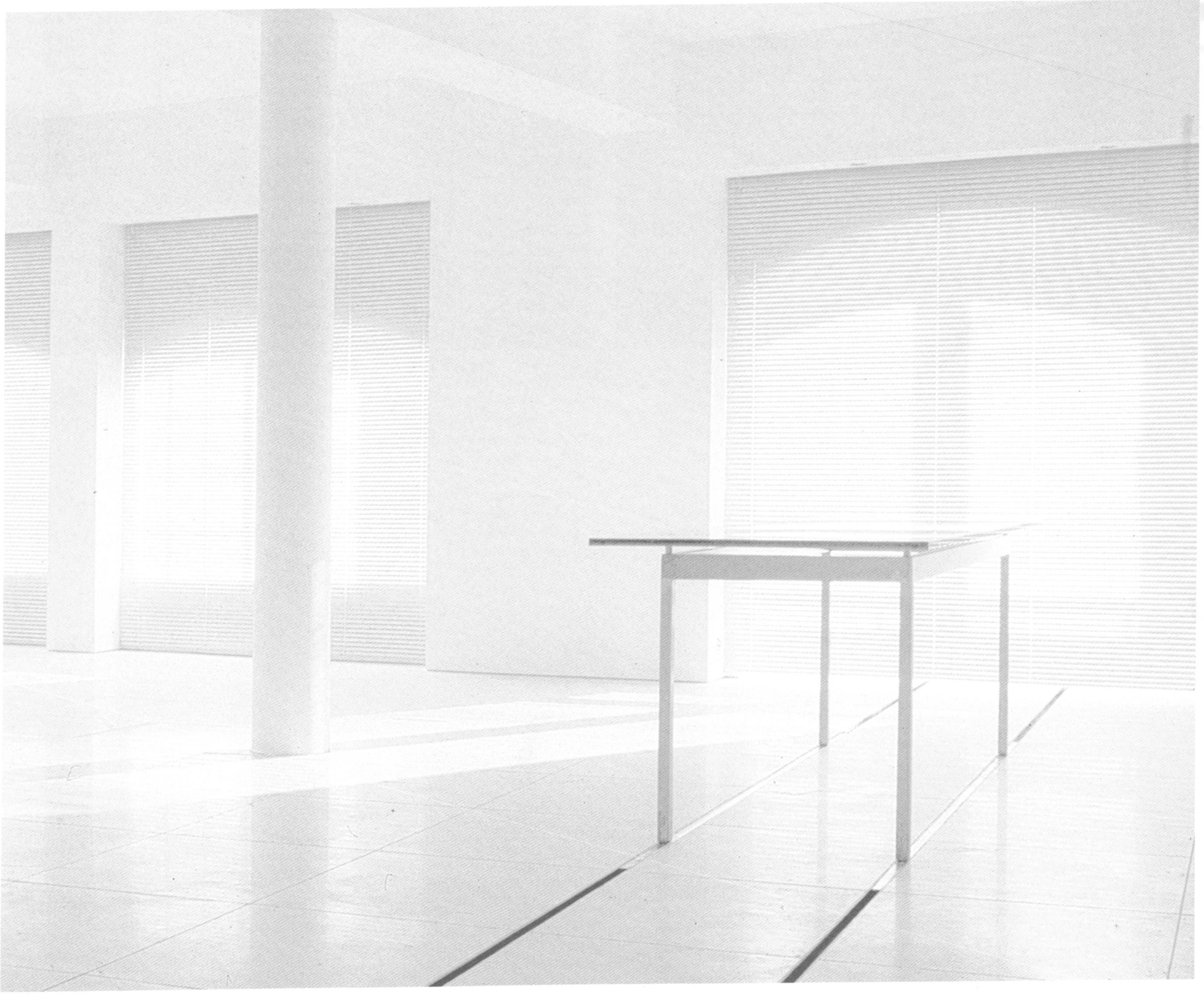

Pallot Flat

Architects Cristina and Alexandre Negoescu's commission was for the design of a residence on one of the floors of a typically Haussmannian nineteenth century Parisian building. The client, an antique dealer by profession, is a collector of works of art as well as curios, and thus required plenty of space for storage and display. The layout also called for a library in which to do research and a large sitting room for social gatherings.

It was decided to endow each room with a distinctive atmosphere, combining in a single flat different, almost clashing architectural and decorative styles. The unity of the home lies in the care and the originality with which all the elements of the residence were designed, from the furniture to the drapery to the carpentry. Moreover, the work benefited from the collaboration of prestigious craftsmen capable of materializing perfectly the architects' desires.

The sitting room recreates a classic atmosphere typical of the nineteenth century. The antique furniture, the large drapes, the carpets and the shelves and walls are covered in velvet fixed with golden tacks, creating a sombre space lit with candelabra and small lamps that take the visitor back in time. The office is similarly inspired by the libraries of the eighteenth century.

The dining room boasts Art Deco furnishings and finishes. A large shell-shaped lamp illuminates walls covered in varied shades of gold leaf. The table, designed and built expressly for this project, can be lengthened by means of an elegant metal device to accommodate large dinner parties.

In the kitchen, the bedroom and the bathroom loud colours typical of sixties and seventies decor were employed. Motifs drawn from Pop aesthetics distinguish the flooring of these rooms. The bedroom ceiling includes, moreover, plaster panels and colored backgrounds that yield an original geometric pattern. Color plays a leading role as well in the dressing room, where the wardrobe doors were painted with red, blue, yellow and pink trim.

Despite the medley of diverse styles, and of materials as dissimilar as velvet, silk, wood, plaster and plastic, the Pallot flat strikes one as a residence of coherent proportions in which the finishes coexist in equilibrium.

Each room of the residence has its own style and recreates different stylistic trends from very different periods.

The gold leaf that covers the dining room walls and ceiling endows the room with uniform luminosity. As in the libraries of yesteryear, the office lamps provide spotlighting for reading.

The dining room table is a highly elegant work of craftsmanship. With its metal mechanism and additional wooden leaf, the table can be lengthened to accommodate large dinner parties.

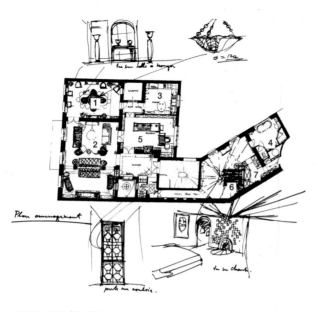

Sketch of the floor plan

1. Dining room
2. Sitting room
3. Kitchen
4. Bathroom
5. Office
6. Bedroom
7. Dressing room

Below are the most notable details of the project, such as the dining room lamp or the hall doors.

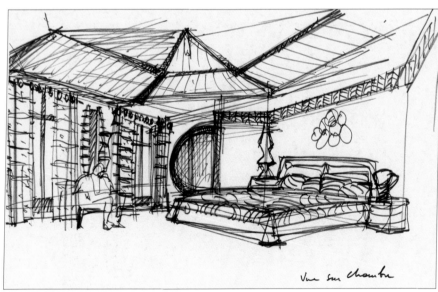

Sketch of the bedroom

Sketch of the bathroom

Sketch of the sitting room

Architects: Cristina & Alexandre Negoescu

Collaborators: Atelier Meriguet Carrere (decorative

paintwork), Barbu Nitescu (sculpture), Atelier

Phelippeau Tapissier (upholstery), Léopold Andreu

(sculpture and fibre optics) and Martine Klotz

(lighting).

Built: 2001

Location: Paris, France

Gross floor area: 2.040 sq. ft.

Photography: Mihail Moldoveanu

Photograph on page 168: John Bennet

House Over the Water

The site chosen to develop this project lies on the Seattle waterfront, amid the city's floating houses. Its particular location conditioned the design by the Jennifer Randall studio: although on one hand they had to deal with harsh climatic factors, such as humidity, strong winds and salt air, on the other hand they had the advantage of the magnificent views of the bay and special luminosity characteristic of the area.

The stunning imagination of the designers coupled with the inestimable enthusiasm of the clients engendered original, heterodox spaces infused with a sense of humor. Almost all the walls and partitions were painted in vivid colors that contrast with and at the same time complement the numerous works of art and curios in the owners' collection.

The common rooms are distributed on two levels: the ground floor accommodates the kitchen, the dining room and a spacious double-height sitting room with a large window over Elliot Bay. The furnishings combine such classic pieces as chairs by Charles and Ray Eames with elements designed by the architects themselves, such as the cupboards. Even the kitchen, in general an eminently practical space, has been instilled with fantasy by equipping it with appliances from a variety of collections.

On the first floor are the bedrooms and their respective bathrooms, all painted with broad colored trim. Additionally, phrases and words were inscribed on some walls in elegant, elongated lettering, in an act of poetic reference. The halls not only connect rooms but also serve as display spaces for drawings, paintings, masks and other souvenirs from the family's travels.

The structural system of the house consists of bearing walls, painted steel beams and a pitched roof with wooden beam fill. Some rooms feature small exposed trusses which, in addition to their structural role, support the varied lighting elements.

The originality of the interior resides in the vivid colors of the walls and the collection of curious objects.

Architects: Jennifer Randall & Associates

Built: 2000

Location: Seattle, USA

Gross floor area: 2,903 sq. ft.

Photography: Jordi Miralles

Photograph on page 178: Chris Gascoigne/View

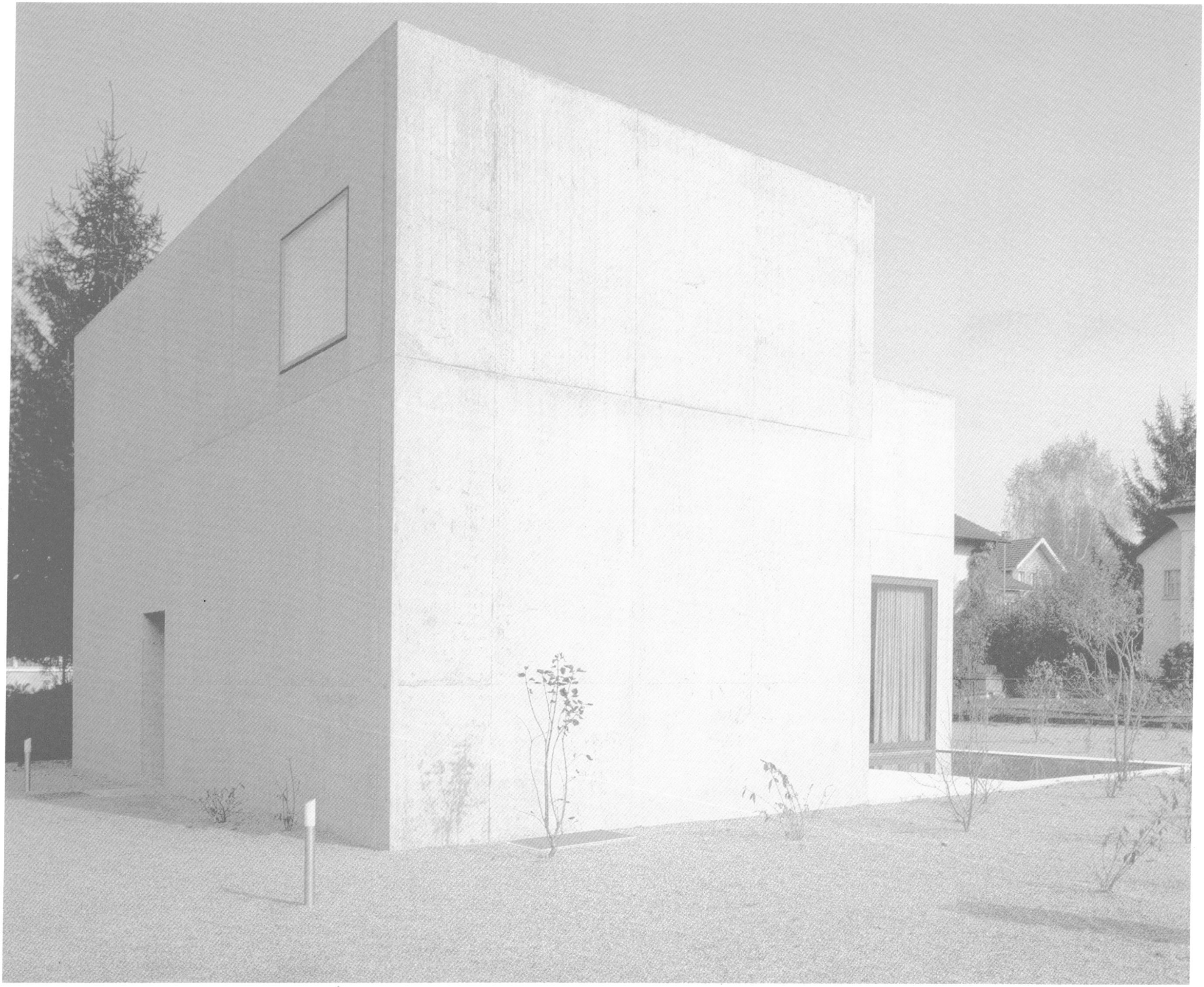

Olabuenaga House

The Italian architect Ettore Sottsass designed this single-family residence, currently owned by the Acme Studios company, using as a reference the light and the shadows of the island of Maui, where it is located. The house was built atop a hill with magnificent views of the sea.

The structural system of the building consists of a black roof slab supported on two slender columns of the same color anchored to the ground. Under this roof, which looks like a large table, were placed a number of independent blocks of different shapes, materials and colors. Sottsass has always relied on color in creating singular architectural universes, of which this house is a magnificent example.

The entrance is defined by an arched door, painted bright red, which leads to an interior of serene lines that contrast with the eccentricity of the façades. On the ground floor are the common the spaces —the sitting room, the dining room, the kitchen and a study— with the entire floor covered in American oak, underscoring the spatial continuity. The sitting room is enclosed by a façade with large spans of glass, affording abundant views and light.

So as not to cut off the interior from the outside environment, no curtains were used in the windows of the house. Nonetheless, to avoid glare, the differences in height and size of the blocks that make up the building ensure that all rooms are shaded: the sitting room, for example, is protected by the shadow cast by the body of the bedroom.

The stairway to the first floor is also of oak, with white-painted tubular metal banisters. This level was reserved for the bedrooms, each with its own bathroom. The floor is covered with wool carpeting, interrupted at the bathrooms, which are finished in small white ceramic tiles.

Most of the furnishings —the sitting room and dining room tables for instance— were also designed by Sottsass. The kitchen furnishings and the bookshelves in the study were designed specifically for the project. The colors are the same as those of the façades.

The slope of the lot was resolved by building a large platform upon which the house sits.

As each room was built with different materials, sidings and colors, the differentiation between the domestic functions of the spaces can be seen from outside. A good example of this is the south façade, where the sitting room is entirely glassed-in and the bedroom has square windows cut out of a solid white-painted enclosure.

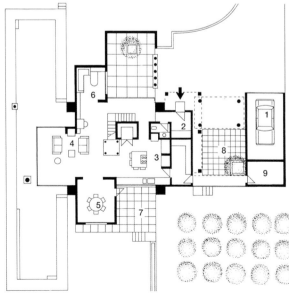

Ground floor

1. Garage
2. Entrance
3. Kitchen
4. Sitting room
5. Dining room
6. Study
7. Terrace
8. Courtyard
9. Workshop

0 1 2

The shelves, which hold a collection of radios, and the centerpiece of the kitchen, serving as an improvised dining space, were designed in black-painted wood specifically for the project. Both elements stand out in an interior of soft shades.

Architect: Ettore Sottsass

Collaborator: Johanna Grawunder

Opened: 1998

Location: Maui, Hawai, USA

Gross floor area: 2,680 sq. ft.

Photography: Undine Pröhl

Photograph on page 184: Ruedi Walti

Tow Studios **Loft in Tribeca**

minimalist

Flat in Sant Sadurní

This flat fuses architecture and decoration to create a complex, functional space. Both disciplines are reflected simultaneously such that it becomes difficult to decide which elements respond to structural requirements, which are functional and which are purely decorative. Essence and ornamentation are inseparable and necessary in giving meaning to this dwelling. In developing the project, the architect drew deeply on improvisation: not that decisions were taken at random, rather the work progressed on the basis of previously selected options with new designs emerging from reflection upon what was already in place.

In addition to the construction and furnishings, special care was taken with the finishes, particularly the paintwork. Each area boasts its own shades that highlight different details. The wall fittings, for example, stand out against the rest of the wall. On the other hand, some walls bear inscriptions which play a dual role: one semantic and the other visual. In addition, the paint serves to dissimulate textures: thus the brick is blurred in different pastel shades and the wood vanishes behind gold.

Even the stairway changes character as it rises. The first step is wood, a sort of introduction followed by two treads of exposed concrete which afford the structure solidness, then the ensemble transforms into a malleable metal plate rising in folds up to the wooden loft. This element is a compendium of the ideas governing the project: a mix of construction details, materials, colors, textures and finishes comprising a heterogeneous whole while producing manifold sensations which enrich one's perception of the ambience.

The lighting for the flat was resolved in a number of ways. On one hand, sunlight enters through windows of varying transparency, treated glass of different textures and opacity. On the other hand, there are numerous lamps: floor lamps casting diffused light; table lamps for specific points; and some which are almost purely decorative, providing only referential light.

Some of the partitions are decorated with typographic inscriptions of varying colors and sizes.

The originality of this project lies in its sincerity. No gimmicks are employed to conceal the fittings, the surfaces are treated to accentuate the textures and the mostly doorless cupboards show off their contents. The space gives the perception of being somewhat chaotic yet candid and spontaneous.

Tearing out the first floor partitions helped to conceive the space in broader terms. The walls are composed of small wooden panels painted in different colors. Another strategy for separating the spaces was the introduction of several levels.

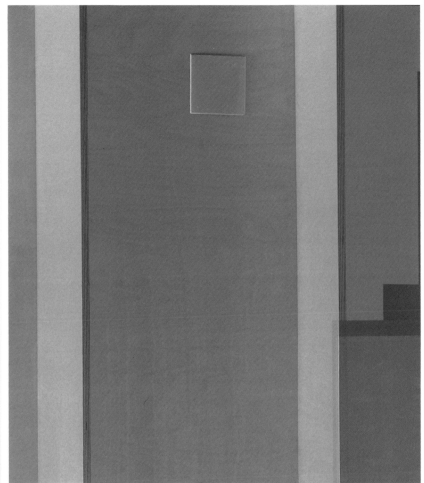

Architect: Josep Juvé

Location: Sant Sadurní, Spain

Built: 1999

Gross floor area: 1,075 sq. ft.

Photography: Eugeni Pons

Photograph on page 192: Björg Photography

Austintonian House

Michael Czysz, Achitröpolis

Dubbed the master of maximalism by some specialist media, Michael Czysz has become a driving force behind stylistic blending. Although his career originally fed on minimalism, the needs and demands of his extravagant clients have come to shape a peculiar style in which myriad materials and shapes coexist. The latest residential project to emerge from his Architröpolis studio represented a new challenge for the company, resulting in the design of a futuristic home of organic shapes. A huge ellipsoidal platform raised above ground level bears two blocks, patios and a large pool. An oval-shaped volume houses the common areas: a spacious sitting room with sofas designed by the architects themselves, the kitchen and the dining room. The bedroom, with corresponding bathroom and dressing room, is located in the other, smaller circular construction. The roof, a large slab that projects out from the façades to create a sheltered outdoor area, stresses the curvy lines of the blocks and lends the project an aerodynamic look.

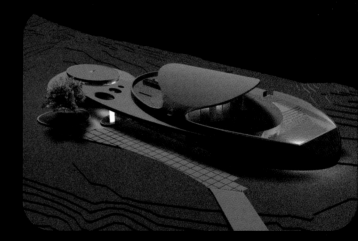

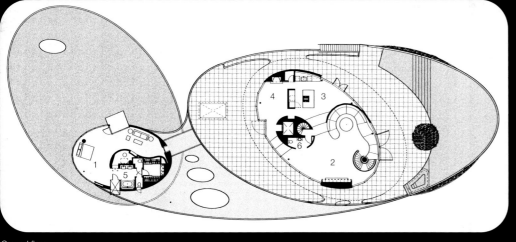

1. Master bedroom
2. Sitting room
3. Kitchen
4. Dining room
5. Bathroom
6. Dressing room

Ground floor

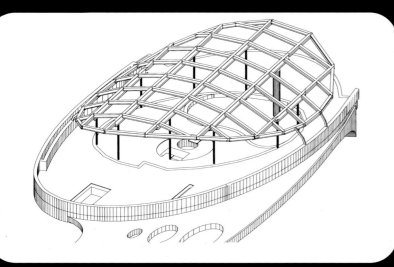

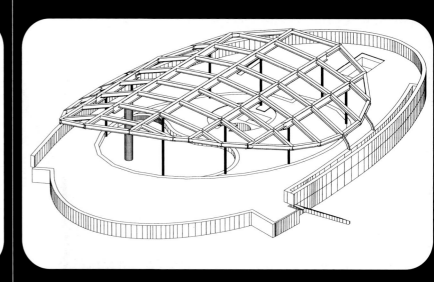

Perspectives of the structural system

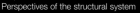

Architects: Michael Czysz, Architröpolis

Sand, of Pocci Dondoli for Desalto.

Tururú, of Teresa Sepulcre for Tes.

Maximalist furniture

Falling just short of excess, the new designs opt to shed the shyness and frigidity which ruled the nineties in favor of near-reckless abandon. Copious doses of imagination and a feeling quite the opposite of formal austerity define many of the latest proposals in furniture design. After a decade dominated by simplicity and plain, near-invisible lines, the coldness of steel and glass and the neutrality of white, a departure from minimalism arises coupled with a carefree approach to exaggeration, ostentation and a taste for well-conceived excess.

Furniture design has become a discipline open to all sorts of influences and changes affecting society, and these changes now point to a striking maximalist style, leaving behind formal subtlety and discretion.

It is early yet to speak of a generalized trend, what with numerous sectors of the market still adhering to "less is more" —defended in his day by Mies van der Rohe and championed in the nineties by designers and architects who took his words to their final consequences. Now, however, exaggeration is gaining ground apace; fatuousness and luxury are back to stay.

Exuberance materializes in uninhibited, generous and on occasion impossible shapes. Fresh, vivid and whimsical shades color the designs, and dress them in textures as pleasant as they are surprising, at the same time new, and until recently, unthinkable, materials are favored for their craftsmanship.

These designs wear their expressiveness with pride: daring, bold, spontaneous shapes abounding in personality; elements whose lines scorn the risk of experimentation and defy the rules to the point that we surrender to their sublime, genuine singularity.

Karpousi, for Valais.

Zamaroli Fingerprint, for Valais.

Table Light, by Nick Crosbie for Inflate Ltd.

Design, by Marc Newson.

Droog Lacet, by Marcel Wanders Studio. photo: Maarten Van Houten

Hänsgrum, by Michael Koenig.

Euroasia, by Soichiro Kanbayashi for Dilmos.

Paragaudi, by Ingo Mauer.

207

Omni, by Karim Rashid for Galerkin.

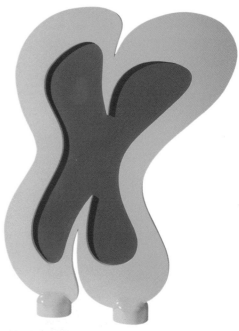

No mires, by Teresa Sepulcre for Tes.

Bum-Bum, by Teresa Sepulcre for Tes.

Chiqui-Chiqui, by Teresa Sepulcre for Tes.

Lounge Chair, by Nick Crosbie for Inflate Ltd.

Eggvases, by Marcel Wanders Studio. photo: Maarten Van Houten

Spongeva, by Marcel Wanders Studio.photo: Maarten Van Houten

Voyager Nest, for Saporiti Italia.

Qual Mazzolin di Fiori, by Bertozzi & Dal Monte Casoni for Dilmos.

Locations and directory

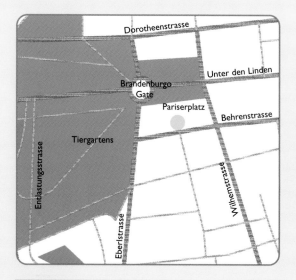

DZ Bank

Pariserplatz 3, Berlin, Germany

Gehry Partners, LLP

keithm@foga.com   **14**

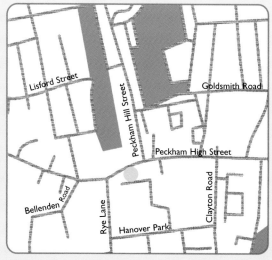

Peckham Library

122 Peckham Hill Street, London, UK

Alsop & Stormer

www.alsoparchitects.com   **24**

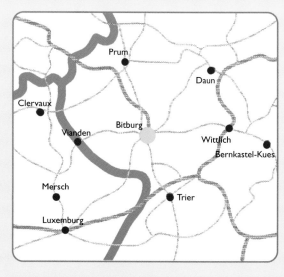

Vocational Training Center

Henri-Dunant Strasse 1, Bitburg, Germany

Behnisch & Partner

bp@behnisch.com   **36**

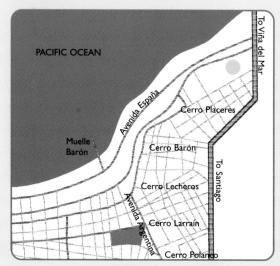

Expansion of the Architecture School

Avenida España 1680, Valparaíso, Chile

LWPAC

olang@lwpac.net   **42**

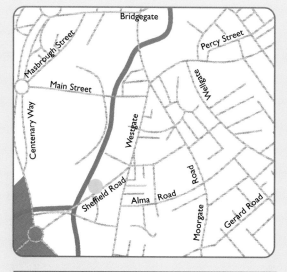

Magna Science Museum

Sheffield Road, Templeborough, Rotherham, UK

Wilkinson Eyre Architects

www.wilkinsoneyre.com   **52**

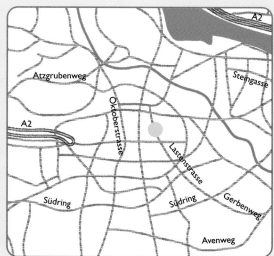

Hypo Alpe Adria Bank

Alpen Adria Platz 1, Klagenfurt, Austria

Morphosis

m.johnson@morphosis.net   **58**

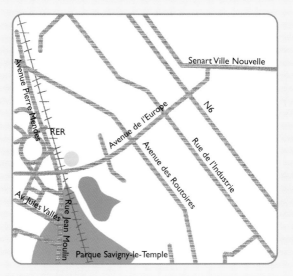

Café Musiques
Avenue de l'Europe 301, Savigny-le-Temple, France
Périphériques
soa@club-internet.fr   **66**

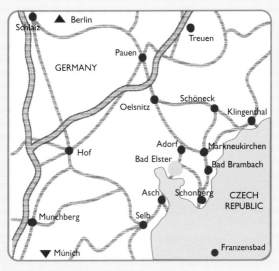

Spa Bad Elster
Bad Strasse 6, Bad Elster, Germany
Behnisch & Partner
bp@behnisch.com   **72**

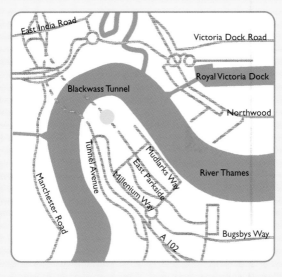

Mind Zone
Millenium Dome, Greenwich Peninsula, London, UK
Zaha Hadid Architects
gayle@zaha-hadid.com   **82**

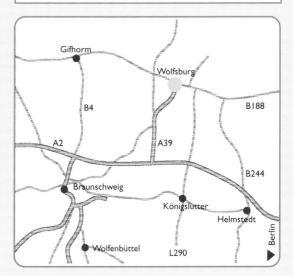

The Lounge
Porsche Strasse 53, Wolfsburg, Germany
Zaha Hadid Architects
gayle@zaha-hadid.com   **90**

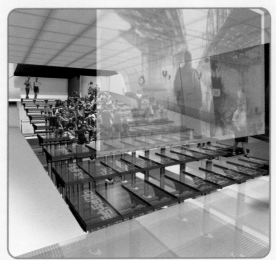

Museum of Art and Technology
New York, USA
Leeser Architecture
www.leeser.com   **100**

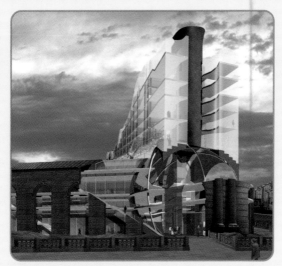

Queens Museum of Art-New Holland Cultural Center
Eric Owen Moss
www.ericowenmoss.com   **104**

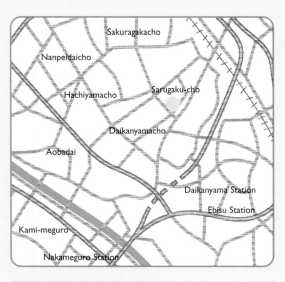

Boutique Christian Lacroix

24-4 Sarugaku-cho, Shibuya-ku, Tokyo, Japan

Caps Architects

elockard@caps-architects.com

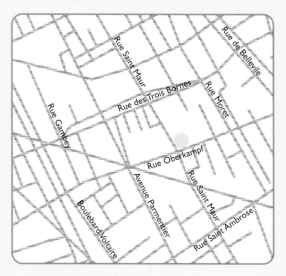

Café Charbon/Nouveau Casino

Rue Oberkampf 109, Paris, France

Périphériques

soa@club-internet.fr

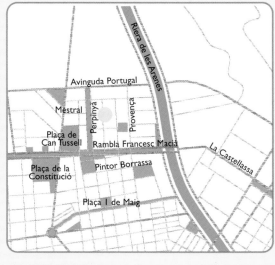

Hotel Woman

Perpinyà 17, Terrassa, Spain

Lola Lago

www.lolalagointeriores.com

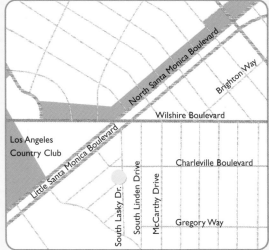

Hotel Maison 140

140 South Lasky Drive, Beverly Hills, CA, USA

Tolkin & Associates

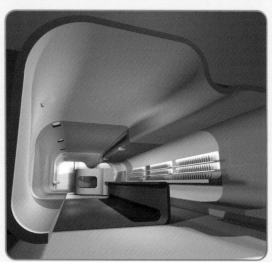

Glass, Bot and Pod

New York, USA

Leeser Architecture

www.leeser.com

MTV Networks Headquarters

26th Street and Colorado Boulevard, Santa Monica, CA, USA

Felderman & Keatinge Associates

www.fkadesign.com

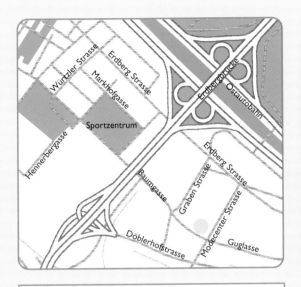